MONEY MATTERS

A Modern Pilgrim's Economic Progress

MONEY MATTERS

A Modern Pilgrim's Economic Progress

Edward Holloway

THE SHERWOOD PRESS

First published 1986

© Edward Holloway 1986

The Sherwood Press Ltd, 88 Tylney Road, London E7 0LY

ISBN 0 907671 21 7

Typeset in Times by BookEns, Saffron Walden
Printed and bound by Redwood Burn Ltd, Trowbridge, Wiltshire

CONTENTS

LIST OF PLATES

Between pages 104 and 105

The author's birth certificate
Parents
Early days in Rovno with family and friends
Passport for travelling in Russia in 1909
The author in his office at 26 Grosvenor Place (1937)
Vincent Cartwright Vickers (1939)
Parliamentary candidate (1945)
Sr Ian MacTaggart
Patrick de Laszlo
Damon de Laszlo
The author in his later years

FOREWORD

The proofs of *Money Matters* arrived on the day that Edward Holloway died. He had been a good friend of mine for over forty years and I have been associated with many of his projects during those years. Edward's work for a sane monetary system goes back to the depression of the 1930s. He aimed at an economic utopia but was a realist, and, when people 'pinched his clothing', he was delighted that the fruits of his research were being used to further the aims he had so much at heart. When he talked about what he had achieved in half a century of voluntary work he was very modest about his own input, but I am aware, and so are many of his friends, that his influence on other people, people with more power than he, was significant and all this work was done without expecting rewards of any sort.

There is still much to be done to achieve sane monetary systems in the world and it is to be hoped that this work will go on through the aegis of the Economic Research Council — that would be Edward Holloway's best memorial.

John Paxton

Bruton, Somerset
December 1985

1

HOW IT ALL STARTED

Looking back over the past fifty years it is still a matter of some amazement to me that for the greater part of my life I have been closely involved with questions of economic and monetary policy. Had I been asked in the 1920s what I knew about economics I should have truthfully replied 'absolutely nothing'. I subsequently found that this was by no means an unusual state of affairs and that this ignorance was shared by the majority of the population, including MPs, industrialists and others.

There was nothing in my early life to indicate that I would be closely concerned with economic questions. My father was employed by the Indo-European Telegraph Company, and at the time when I was born, in 1906, he was stationed in a small town in Russia, near the Polish frontier, called Rovno. This was a relay station between Warsaw and Odessa on the Black Sea coast. The Indo-European Telegraph Company operated a direct overland telegraph line from London to Karachi via Tehran in Persia (or Iran, as it is today), and many of its staff were stationed in Russia and Persia. My father died in Rovno when I was quite young and, after staying in Odessa with an uncle and aunt for some months, my mother returned to England with my sister and myself.

I do not remember very much about these very early days in my life, though I do recall a tremendous storm in Rovno, when hailstones as big as golf balls smashed all the windows in our house. Also, in Odessa, my uncle took me to the Black Sea coast and I saw men and women bathing with nothing on, but on separate parts of the shore. Subsequently I told my very Victorian grandmother about this, and she summed it up in one word—'disgusting'. I still wonder what was disgusting about it.

I have a rather splendid birth certificate, issued in Odessa

which shows my date of birth as 13 and 26 July 1906. For
many years I have tried to cash in on having two birthdays, but
signally failed. One friend does, however, send me a greetings
card on my Russian birthday!

The Indo-European Telegraph Company was one of the
pioneers in the telegraph communications business. My family
had close connections with this company, and my uncle was
stationed in Sukhum on the Black Sea coast when the Russian
Revolution broke out and he and his family were marooned
from 1917 until they were rescued in 1919.

The Indo line operated from 18 Old Broad Street in the City
of London via North Walsham, then by cable to Emden and
from there an overhead telegraph line through Berlin; Warsaw;
Rovno (later Berdichev); Odessa; Sukhum; Tiflis; and Tabriz
to Tehran. From then on to Karachi it was operated by the
Indo-European Telegraph Department, one line going through
the Persian Gulf.

The Indo line was closed down when war broke out in 1914,
the staff working for the war period with the Eastern Telegraph
Company, with whom the Indo Company had a joint purse
agreement. When the line re-opened after the war it was largely
operated with pre-war equipment, Wheatstone transmitters
which had to be wound up like a grandfather clock, stick per-
forators to punch out the dots and dashes on tape and so on. I
believe that the late Mr Stratford Andrews, one-time Managing
Director, was the inventor of the porcelain insulator which
made possible the carrying of overhead lines for such a long dis-
tance. It was said that these insulators were a favourite target
for Persian tribesmen, who could not resist taking pot-shots at
them, leading to grave interruptions in communications. The
Persian government then issued a decree that anyone caught
doing this would have his ears cut off and nailed to the nearest
telegraph pole!

There are many fascinating stories to be told about this and
similar enterprises, and they deserve better chronicling than
they have so far been given.

I joined the Indo Company in 1922 when it re-opened after
the First World War with the youthful expectation of spending
much of my time overseas. This idea attracted me very much,

but in 1925 the Indo was swallowed up by a merger with Imperial and International Communications, later Cable and Wireless. One thing my short experience working in this field brought home to me was the value in human terms of the smaller company, where the relationship between the individuals who worked together were on a much better basis. This was demonstrated by the fact that fifty years after the company closed down the staff still met at an annual dinner in London, and even today they keep in touch through a circular letter sent to the remaining few.

The merger which took place in 1925 meant that the closely knit Indo staff were swallowed up in a much larger and more impersonal concern. This brought my first realisation that economic forces, completely outside my control, could materially alter my future. My interest in telegraph communications as a career progressively declined as a result of this experience.

The Indo Company had a rather enlightened approach to employment conditions. A 36-hour week was worked and, although these were performed round the clock (unsocial hours they call them now) it left quite a lot of time when other interests could be pursued. I attempted, with a colleague, to build up an importing business for motor accessories, starting with the import of a car-theft device called the Guardsman. These were shipped from the USA and the firm concerned gave us sole rights in the UK. We set up agencies in various parts of the country and arranged for publicity in the motoring press. Our first consignment arrived, and with great hopes we distributed the supply to our agents. But it was 1931 and Britain went off the gold standard. The cost of importing from the USA became prohibitive and subsequently we had to close down with a loss of our investment. This was my second lesson in economics, and I realised that I had not the foggiest notion of the reasons for all this happening. I began to read and study the subject a little more closely.

Perhaps the most influential factor which led to my life taking a new direction was the impact of unemployment. Although not affected personally, no-one could fail to be concerned at the level of unemployment which so gravely disrupted the lives of so many of our fellow-countrymen. By 1931 the unemployment figures had reached nearly 3 million, the dole was quite inadequate and those who were unemployed not only suffered from a lack of nourishment for themselves and their families but also the gradual erosion of their self-confidence and self-respect.

One experience stands out very clearly in my mind. With some friends associated with the Rover Scout Movement we had formed a Concert Party which we called 'The Nondescripts'. We occasionally gave shows to help deserving causes, and as a result we were invited to give a performance in a disused church in the Grays Inn Road, London. Up to 400 so-called 'down and outs' assembled every night to seek shelter and were given a couple of newspaper posters on which to sleep on the floor. Bread, cheese and cocoa were doled out and the atmosphere was one of extreme doom and gloom.

In these circumstances it was not easy to perform our usual light entertainment, and the audience only came to life in a sketch purporting to be in Dartmoor Prison! However, when we had finished our show, we talked to some of the men who were from a surprisingly diverse background. Some were craftsmen and ex-professional men who had come down in the world. Others were clearly from the working class, but all were depressed and hopeless as to their prospects for the future.

Going home on the bus afterwards, I have never known my colleagues so silent and thoughtful.

I had been concerned to do what I could to alleviate some of the suffering and misery and gave help to the SOS Society, who did much good work among the down-and-outs in London. Among other things I begged old clothes from my friends and had them collected for distribution to those desperately needing them. But I was vaguely dissatisfied with this kind of activity, which at best was only a palliative and did not in any way get to the root of the problem. It was also borne upon me that, while I helped in collecting old clothes, people capable of making and supplying them were themselves out of work. At the same time food was being destroyed and its production restricted. Milk was being poured down drains while children starved. Bankruptcies and forced sales were the order of the day and many other absurdities abounded. But when one asked why, no satisfactory answer was forthcoming, whether from the Government and other official sources. The only solution seemed to be to tighten our belts, and we had to accept a 10 per cent cut in wages and salaries to save the country. It all seemed like living in a madhouse.

It was in 1931 that I came in touch with an Irish author named Eimar O'Duffy, and we spent many hours with likeminded friends in discussing the political and economic scene. O'Duffy, who had written several satirical works, including *The Spacious Adventures of the Man in the Street, King Goshawk and the Birds, Asses in Clover* and other books which had commanded considerable attention in the literary world, was at this time engaged in writing a new book which he claimed would give the answers to the unsolved problems which we found so baffling.

When we tried to pump him as to the contents he would only say 'Wait until my book is published, then you will find the answer.'

I am afraid we took this with a grain of salt, and ragged him unmercifully, referring to his meetings with colleagues in the Leisure Society which met occasionally as 'The Committee for Public Safety'. We lost no opportunity of assuring him that we doubted his ability to provide an answer to the problems which seemed to baffle all the experts in the country. His constant reply—'read my book when it is published'—became something of a joke.

However, the book was finally published by Putnams in 1932. Entitled *Life and Money*, it was described on the fly-leaf as 'a critical examination of the principles and practice of orthodox economics with a practical scheme to end the muddle it has made to our civilisation'. A bold claim, to say the least!

It so happened that at the time the book was published I took some supplementary leave which had to be taken in the winter months. Staying in an isolated cottage in the country the weather was, to say the least, inclement, and we were practically snowed up for a time. Thus I had the opportunity of studying the book without interruption. And I found it a real

eye-opener. So many of the unsolved questions were elucidated
and the means of solving the nation's problems seemed to be
made crystal-clear.

O'Duffy summarised his views as follows:

> The economic troubles of the world are occasioned by the fact that
> a monetary system which originated at a time when demand for
> goods was greater than the supply, and when competition between
> man and man was inevitable, is still in use at a time when the supply
> of goods is greater than the demand, and competition is giving
> place to co-operation.

There is no doubt that the main case made in *Life and Money*
profoundly affected my own thinking on the crisis facing
Britain. Here, at last, was a clear and understandable statement
showing why we had failed to establish the 'land fit for heroes'
promised by Lloyd George after the First World War. Here
was shown the reason why men women and children suffered
from malnutrition while the production of goods and services
was restricted and much of the output of farm and factory failed
to find a buyer. The idea began to form in my mind that something must be done to focus attention on the, to me, obvious
solution.

It is true that some of O'Duffy's views would have been modified in the light of subsequent events, but, by and large, the
book can still be read with profit and contains much that is valid
even fifty years after publication.

With what now seems a rather naive view of political affairs I
believed that these ideas had only to be publicised and brought
to the attention of the powers-that-be to bring about the far-
reaching changes in economic and monetary policy that the
nation so sorely needed.

Another incident which occurred during this early period of
activity, and which had a considerable influence on my thinking, was at a small meeting held one Sunday afternoon at the
Trinity College Oxford Mission in Stratford Road, Stratford,
which is in the East End of London. My cousin, the Rev. W. E.
('Pat') Keating, was in charge of this Mission in what was one
of the poorest and most deprived areas of London, and he asked

me to go down to the Mission to talk to a group of unemployed youths who met on Sunday afternoons. They were aged between 16 and 20, none of them had ever had any regular work since leaving school, they appeared to have no hope of ever being employed and they lived a life of degradation and poverty such as is hard to imagine in these more enlightened days.

I talked to them for about 40 minutes, trying to tell them of the possibilities of a better life for them if we succeeded in reforming the money system to enable all that could be produced to be consumed. Somewhat naturally, their reaction showed a bitterness and hostility to those better off than they were, and the natural feeling was to seek to take from the wealthy in an effort to improve their lot. I tried to explain that if we succeeded in putting right the system they could have a better life, without the necessity of taking from those who were already well off.

This seemed to make some impression, and they were obviously interested and wanted to know more about the ideas; at the conclusion one of them said—'When is what you're talking about coming, Mister?'

In fact, it took until the outbreak of war in 1939 to establish the fact that the poverty and misery enforced on these young men and millions like them had been completely unnecessary, for under wartime conditions the orthodox rules of finance no longer applied! Perhaps there is a lesson to be learned from this in 1986!

The question was—how to go about achieving the reforms we sought. I found that in talking to friends about the question it was not too difficult to persuade them that the O'Duffy case had merit, and so we decided to do something about it. I was then living in the Muswell Hill area of north London and, together with some close friends, we formed a society which we called the Prosperity League. Our first meeting was held in the local church hall with an audience of about 30, and we enrolled our first members at a subscription of one shilling per annum.

It was in these early days of the Prosperity League that an incident occurred which at the time did not mean much but has since remained in my memory. I happened to take a friend of mine to see a spiritualist medium in the West End of London.

She wanted to consult about some pressing personal problems. I had no interest in spiritualism, but I offered to drive her to the appointment in my car and arranged to pick her up for lunch afterwards.

When we met for lunch, she seemed rather preoccupied, and I asked her why she was so silent. After a while she said to me, 'Did you know anyone named Cook?' I confessed that I did not know anyone of that name. She then said he had something wrong with his legs. I still had no idea who it might be, but she said that, anyway, she had a message for me; that a man named Cook wanted me to know that he was interested that I was working for monetary reform. He added that had he known about the idea when active here, he would have supported the movement very strongly.

I gathered from my friend that she was very put out by having this message to give me and had nothing to assist her with her own problems. However, I did not know Cook and so forgot all about it. It was only subsequently, when reading about the problems of the miners, that I realised that the message was probably from A. J. Cook, the miners' leader who had suffered some injury to his legs. It all seemed rather improbable, but it still sticks in my memory.

One development which gave us some encouragement arose as a result of a letter I sent to Euan Wallace, the Member of Parliament for Hornsey. It was in his constituency that our inaugural meeting had been held. He had been appointed as a Commissioner for a Distressed Area (later called Special Areas, as distressed was a bit too near the truth). I wrote to him pointing out our belief that the suffering and misery which he must have observed in the course of his work arose from a faulty monetary mechanism which failed in its task of making available what was produced to those in dire need. Poverty in the midst of plenty was then becoming a widely used expression and, as an MP expressly charged with examining this problem, he should pay some attention to our views. As a result of further correspondence, Euan Wallace agreed to meet Alan de V. Leigh, Secretary of the London Chamber of Commerce, who was a well-known critic of the orthodox system.

The upshot of all this was a letter I subsequently received

from Euan Wallace in which he referred me to his report to the House of Commons on the distressed areas, which he said had been considerably altered as a result of our intervention. Later I heard the comment that the only other MP who had understood what he was talking about was Harold Macmillan!

Although the outcome of this effort was not very significant in terms of future government policy, it did, nevertheless, seem to show that if we persevered we might eventually succeed in our efforts to reform the system.

Following this we organised a meeting held in the Essex Hall, London, with Alan de V. Leigh as the speaker and with Vincent C. Vickers, formerly a Director of the Bank of England, in the Chair. The meeting was crowded and was an outstanding success. It brought us into touch with a number of MPs, and thus we began the Pilgrim's Progress towards achieving our aim of reform of the economic and monetary system.

2

PLANS FOR REFORM

The early 1930s saw a considerable upsurge in interest in the need for reform. The statement made by King George V after the breakdown of the Gold Standard in 1931 set the scene for much activity. He said:

> It cannot be beyond the power of man so to use the vast resources of the world as to ensure the material progress of civilisation. No diminution in these resources has taken place. On the contrary, Discovery, Invention, and Organisation have multiplied their possibilities to such an extent that abundance of production has itself created new problems.

The Times, in a leading article in November 1932 asked 'What is the explanation that the farmers and the manufacturers cannot exchange their products, that food is unsaleable, while millions of factory workers are idle and starving, and that the farmer has to go without the goods which they should be employed in making?'

This is just the question we ourselves were asking and the answer seemed quite obvious. In April 1934 a letter appeared in *The Times* which summarised what we felt about the situation. It was signed by a number of influential people, and it stated:

> The present monetary system, the proper function of which is to facilitate that production of goods and their distribution to consumers, has broken down, both in its national and international aspects. The system has become a hindrance to the effective distribution of goods . . . A system must be established under which the issue and recall of currency and credit will be regulated on a national, rational, and scientific basis, so that the correct number of money-tokens shall be available to consumers, to enable them to enjoy the output of production . . .

Other letters followed in similar vein. All this gave us encouragement to go ahead with our efforts to promote the idea of monetary reform. Little did I then realise that fifty years later I would still be engaged in an effort to persuade the authorities of the validity of our diagnosis!

It did not take us long to find out that we were by no means alone in this effort to establish a more realistic approach to economic and monetary questions. For example, we came into touch with the Social Credit movement, founded on the writings of Major C. H. Douglas. Naturally, we sought to establish some co-operation with what proved to be a widespread movement. While we recognised the great contribution which Major Douglas had made, we found to our dismay that the movement supporting him was unprepared to associate with anybody who did not accept the Douglas analysis in its entirety.

One of the supporters of Douglas Social Credit was A. R. Orage. When I first met him he was Editor of the *New English Weekly*. Orage was not unaware of the failings of the Social Credit supporters, and one of his letters to me said that the 'Social Credit movement should be thoroughly ashamed of itself', a sentiment which I came to share.

Orage had a great capacity for encouraging young and aspiring would-be writers, and I found his *New English Weekly* a source of much inspiration. I visited his tiny office in Cursitor Street, off Fetter Lane, quite often. He died after making a brilliant broadcast on the BBC, setting out the case for monetary reform.

In fact, we found that followers of Douglas were adamant that they alone had the solution to the problem. It became almost a religion among the Social Credit groups that Douglas alone was right and only the adoption of his scheme in its entirety could achieve the results we all desired.

We were not at all convinced by his $A+B$ theorem with the attendant adoption of the 'Just Price' and 'National Dividend', and we felt that rigid adherence to the detailed letter of the proposals would militate against their being acceptable by the authorities.

My own feelings were reinforced by the reaction of a number of prominent Conservative politicians at a conference held at

Palace Chambers. This had been arranged to consider whether the case for monetary reform was valid. Major Douglas had been invited but at the last minute refused to attend. The advocacy of the Social Credit viewpoint was left to the Dean of Canterbury, Dr Hewlett Johnson (later known as the 'Red Dean'), then an enthusiastic supporter of Douglas. My sole contribution to the discussion was to appeal to those present that we should not restrict our consideration to the Social Credit scheme, but that we should widen our scope to the need for reform of the monetary system. Unfortunately, this plea was ignored, and the Treasury expert present began to tear holes in the Social Credit scheme as propounded by Dr Johnson. The discussion became more and more complicated in the detailed examination of the Social Credit case, and the Conservative politicians went away obviously bemused by the technicalities and complications which had dominated the conference.

The Social Credit scheme was not the only plan for reform under discussion at that time. One of the leading exponents of monetary reform was Professor Frederick Soddy, FRS. In 1902 he had been associated with Lord Rutherford in the discovery of the Theory of Atomic Disintegration with its vast implications for development of atomic energy in both peace and war. He was awarded the Nobel Laureate Prize in Chemistry for 1921 and he held many posts of high distinction.

The contribution to monetary reform made by Professor Soddy arose from his conviction that the explosive condition of the world arose directly as a result of the existing monetary system. His proposals for reform, dealt with more fully in Chapter 10, were as follows:

(1) The bank cheque system to be altered so that banks keep £ for £ of national money—the whole profits of issue of which have been paid into the public Treasury—against their liabilities to their current account depositors. No private IOU or Promise to Pay to be allowed to take the place of or circulate as legal tender under the penalties applying to counterfeit money.
(2) A purely scientific statistical authority, analogous to the institutions charged with the control of weights and measures

but preferably directly under the Crown, to determine the rate at which new national money is to be issued in order to maintain the price-index of the main commodities, used and used up in living, invariable. This may be termed £'s for lbs, meaning that the same number of £'s have always to be paid for the same number of lbs of the average of the commodities the money is used to buy.

(3) Subject only to the price-index not being thereby raised, the number of £'s of national money issued to be unlimited, whereby the community would be able to repay its debts, £ for £ and lb for lb of what the £ buys, rather than, as now, Shylock's 'pound of flesh nearest the heart'.

(4) The foreign exchanges to be free to adjust themselves in accordance with the actual genuine mutual trade and investment between this and foreign countries, while being under the direct control of the Government through the statistical authority which manages the internal currency, to protect them from speculation and manipulation by short-term operators not engaged in foreign trade at all.

Soddy brought his powerful analytical mind to bear on the study of monetary science which led him to devise his plan which he called the £ for £ scheme.

He was one of a number of advocates that the issue and regulation of the money supply should be in the hands of a statutory independent body which would work scientifically on data readily obtainable. The maintenance of stability in the internal price level would be the single aim, an increase or decrease in the supply of money being the means by which this would be achieved. Soddy was called by some of us 'Professor Porcupine', for he seemed to be a somewhat prickly character until you got to know him. Perhaps it was as a result of this that he failed to get the recognition which he so richly deserved.

Also among the organisations active in the 1930s which deserves special mention was the New Britain Movement. The genius behind its activities was Dimitrije Mitrinović, who had been introduced to the monetary reform idea by A. R. Orage. Although New Britain had a much wider platform than reform of the monetary system, this was an integral part of its campaign. This is shown by the following quotations from one of its pamphlets entitled *New Britain and Money*:

> The mechanism of Distribution in our highly industrialised system is money, which has assumed an enormous and vital significance. The evolution of money, step by step, has waited on the development of production and markets. And vice-versa, with the result that money is the blood stream of civilisation. As the means of exchange and the register of demand, it is vital. Faults in the mechanism of money can dislocate and disorganise production, as it has done. If then, we have conquered the power of making things in abundance, and if further, the means of distributing things when made is money; if individual consumers nevertheless are unable to get hold of the goods, then the fault must IN THE FIRST PLACE, be in the mechanism of distribution, namely, Money.
>
> And that is the actual case. The issue of money under our system is related neither to production nor consumption. Under the private control and issue of the Banks, its primary relation is to profit. This private, anti-social, anti-human interest of those individuals has brought our civilisation to the brink of ruin. Money must be made to serve the interests of Production: and when the needs of Production have been satisfied, it must further be made to serve the interests of Consumption. For the only legitimate end of Production is Consumption.

The New Britain movement arranged many meetings, conferences, and seminars in the 1930s. It also produced a journal entitled *New Britain*, which achieved a wide circulation. It had a house in Gower Street, which they allowed the Economic Reform Club to use, its headquarters being in Richmond. I was invited to visit Mitrinović on several occasions, but unfortunately he was too ill to receive me when I went to Richmond on two visits. He died shortly afterwards.

The 'Free Economy Plan', put forward by Silvio Gesell, also had its supporters, and they, at least, had some experiments to reinforce their claim for attention. In Swanenkirchen in Bavaria and in Woergl in the Austrian Tyrol the Gesell system had been tried out following the First World War. It proved highly successful until stopped by the banking authorities in their respective countries.

Gesell, son of a German father and a French mother, whose

first work—published in 1891—was entitled *Monetary Reform, the Bridge to a Social State*, was concerned to establish the fact that in an economy, goods are the primary factor to which everything else, including money, must be adapted. He challenged the traditional economic doctrine that the volume of production had to adapt itself to the volume of money available, and he advocated the regulation of the volume of money according to the constantly changing volume of production.

Money should not be treated as a commodity and should not hold sway over goods, but must deteriorate as they do. Money must be subjected to the loss to which goods are liable through the necessity of storage. Money would then no longer be superior to goods, they would be equivalent.

Gesell believed that if money was to perform its task of facilitating the exchange of goods and services satisfactorily, notes would be issued in varying denominations which would have printed spaces on the back to which demurrage stamps would be affixed, each space showing the printed date when demurrage fell due.

Gesell called it Freed Money which would lose part of its face value; 5 or 10 per cent annually, at the expense of the holder. The notes would be held at their face value by attaching to them a demurrage stamp. Notes which were not fully stamped to bring them up to their face value would not be regarded as legal tender. Thus, Gesell argued, money would be driven into constant circulation, and at the end of each year fully stamped notes would be exchanged for a new issue.

A National Currency Office would take the place of the Bank of Issue and would stabilise the general level of prices by issuing more money when prices tended to fall and withdraw money when prices tended to rise, thus establishing the direct relationship between money and goods.

Another interesting and very forthright character we came into contact with was Arthur Kitson, who died in 1937 at the age of seventy-six. He had spent forty years of his life arguing the case for reform of the monetary system. As an engineer and inventor of the first rank he had a claim to be heard. Among his many inventions was the 'Kitson Light', which became known as 'The Mariner's Friend', and he made this freely available to the lighthouse authorities of Great Britain. He was a pioneer in this field and had much to do with the lighting of the Trans-Siberian Railway and other railways in Asia and Europe. He was granted hundreds of patents for inventions covering many branches of engineering.

From 1893 Kitson forthrightly condemned an economic system based on debt and usury as both unsound and morally wrong. He was one of the very few industrialists who was invited to give evidence to the Cunliffe Currency Committee, which was composed of banking interests under the Presidency of Lord Cunliffe, then Governor of the Bank of England, and he submitted long and detailed criticisms of the Interim Report published in August 1918. In the final report of the Committee no attempt was made to answer any of the criticisms put forward by Arthur Kitson. Instead, it reaffirmed support for the policy of deflation and a return to the gold standard. The suicidal results of the acceptance of this policy led to the return to the gold standard in 1925 with its disastrous effect on the economy.

In a notable speech on the Budget proposals in the House of Commons in 1932 Sir Winston Churchill had this to say about the decision which he took in 1925 as Chancellor of the Exchequer to return to the gold standard:

> When I was moved by many arguments and forces in 1925 to return to the gold standard I was assured by the highest experts, and our experts are men of great ability and indisputable integrity and sincerity . . . that we were anchoring ourselves to reality and stability; and I accepted their adivce. I take for myself and my colleagues of other days whatever degree of blame and burden there may be for having accepted their advice. But what has happened? We have had no reality, no stability. The price of gold has risen since then by more than 70 per cent. That is as if a 12-inch foot rule had suddenly been stretched to 19 or 20 inches, as if the pound avoir-dupois had suddenly become 23 or 24 ounces instead of—how much is it?—16. Look at what this has meant to everybody who has been compelled to execute their contracts upon this irrationally enhanced scale. Look at the gross unfairness of such distortion to all producers of real wealth, and to all that labour and science can give us. Look at the enormously increased volume

of commodities which have to be created in order to pay off the same mortgage debt or loan. Minor fluctuations might well be ignored, but I say quite seriously that this monetary convulsion has now reached a pitch where I am persuaded that the producers of new wealth will not tolerate so hideous an oppression.

Are we really going to accept the position that the whole future development of science, our organisation, our increasing co-operation and the fruitful era of peace and goodwill among men and nations; are all these developments to be arbitrarily barred by the price of gold? Is the progress of the human race in this age of almost terrifying expansion to be arbitrarily barred and regulated by for-tuitous discoveries of gold mines here and there or by the extent to which we can persuade the existing cornerers and hoarders of gold to put their hoards again into common stock? Are we to be told that human civilisation and society would have been impossible if gold had not happened to be an element in the composition of the globe?

These are absurdities; but they are becoming dangerous and deadly absurdities. They have only to be asserted long enough, they have only to be left ungrappled with long enough, to endanger that capitalist and credit system upon which the liberties and enjoyments and prosperity, in my belief, of the vast masses depend. I therefore point to this evil and to the search for methods of remedying it as the first, the second and the third of all the prob-lems which should command and rivet our thoughts.

This was a remarkable tribute to those who, like Arthur Kit-son, had opposed the return to gold, only to be overruled by the experts to whom Sir Winston referred. So much that is wrong with our country today stems in no small measure from this fateful decision way back in 1925.

When Arthur Kitson died in 1937 his family arranged for all his writings and records dealing with monetary and economic topics to be sent to me. I thus had the unique opportunity of realising the immense amount of work and effort he had put in over many years in the interests of a saner economic system.

The man who most greatly influenced my early activities in the field of reform was, undoubtedly, Robert Spurrier. His advice and encouragement played a vital part in persuading me to continue the work I had undertaken in a purely voluntary capacity. His faith in my ability to carry out tasks for which I was by no means equipped to undertake was an inspiration which I still recall after so many years.

He played a significant part in the formation of the Economic Reform Club and became its first Chairman in May 1936, a post he held until his death in March 1942. I cannot do better than quote from a Spurrier Memorial Lecture given by Sir Reginald Rowe, then President of the Club in 1943:

> Robert Spurrier was a man of the kindest nature, quiet in manner and entirely unpretentious, with really fine mental qualities— clearness of mind, steady soundess of judgement, an easy command of lucid expression.
>
> Those who knew him could not fail to like and admire him. He did us and our cause yeoman service. And all the time he suffered a severe physical disability without thought of complaint. His life was one of which any man might justly be proud and his death left the world poorer by the loss of a noble character.

An incident which I recall in these early days was the meeting arranged by William Ward with the then Prime Minister, Ramsay Macdonald. William Ward was the founder of the World Brotherhood Federation and was an old friend of Macdonald's. He had become closely associated with our efforts for economic and monetary reform, and made an appointment to see Ramsay to put these ideas before him. He returned from the interview somewhat despondent, for all he could get out of the Prime Minister was 'It's no use talking to me about these ideas, see my son Malcolm,' whereupon the Prime Minister dissolved into tears.

Some time afterwards Malcolm Macdonald made a speech in the House of Commons which made many MPs, even on the Conservative side, speak of him as a possible Prime Minister. This promise faded when Malcolm took up his overseas appointments.

On another occasion I received an urgent summons to go to the House of Commons to meet David Lloyd George, who had asked a great friend of mine, Trystan Edwards, to give him details about his ambitious plan to build a hundred New Towns in Britain. Apparently Lloyd George had undertaken to provide a blueprint of a scheme to deal with the widespread unemployment then prevailing and was desperately seeking every idea he could conjure up to make good his undertaking.

In the autumn of 1934 Lloyd George had set in motion a new economic enquiry and he announced the result as a British New Deal. In March 1935 he received a letter from the Prime Minister, Ramsay Macdonald, challenging Lloyd George to submit his plans for the relief of unemployment and the solving of the economic crisis. This presented Lloyd George with problems for, although he had a broad plan drafted, the detail required to support this had still to be provided, and he was desperately seeking every idea he could conjure up to make good his undertaking to provide a detailed plan for recovery.

Trystan Edwards asked me to accompany him to see Lloyd George in case any question should arise about financing his 100 New Towns scheme, which he had based on monetary reform ideas. In the event, when the question of finance was raised, Lloyd George simply waved his hand and said that Sir Basil Blackett was dealing with all such questions.

Sir Basil had written a book entitled *Planned Money* in 1932 in which he advocated radical changes in monetary policy which he considered were vitally necessary. In this book he asked 'Is twentieth-century Britain content to make continued use of a monetary system which has so conspicuously failed her in the past and is admittedly liable in the future to present her again with the disastrous sequence of boom, slump, boom, slump?' Lloyd George had accepted the view put forward by Sir Basil that 'the nation ought to be able to afford standards of life far higher than it enjoys today, and is baulked of that enjoyment, not because its resources are insufficient, but because they fail to use them rightly.'

Another prominent supporter was Lord Melchett, whose book, *Modern Money*, provided much important material for those interested in reform of the monetary system. In this he wrote: 'There is no economist, no banker, no financier, who can give clear answers put by a distressed and tormented world. The whole of this subject, upon which our very existence depends, is full of doubt and controversy and always has been.' To my mind, if Lloyd George, supported by Sir Basil Blackett and others who understood the money problem, had been given the attention they deserved by the authorities, subsequent history would have been very different. The country would have recovered far sooner from the economic crisis, but the authorities, blinded to all but the orthodox approach, turned it down with the poor excuse that it would be too costly. The price paid in terms of human suffering was not, in the orthodox view, of any account.

3

THE ECONOMIC REFORM CLUB

The multiplicity of plans for reform of the economic and monetary system, some of which have been briefly outlined in the previous chapter, posed considerable problems to those of us who wanted the whole subject re-examined and ventilated. In addition to those mentioned there were a number of other less well-known plans and ideas put forward, for example by Claud Jacobs, W. Wakinshaw, Taylor Peddie, McNair Wilson and many others. We did not see the necessity of supporting one particular scheme. Our view was that plans should be considered at the highest level, and that not one of them supplied the complete answer to Britain's acute economic problems. To us, the task seemed to be to press for an impartial investigation while, in the main, the supporters of individual schemes were adamant that they alone had the correct solution.

Various movements had sprung up, some to support particular plans and others, like the League to Abolish Poverty, founded by William Ward, and the National Credit Association, led by the Marquis of Tavistock (later the Duke of Bedford), were less dogmatic in their approach. Our aim was to bring as many of these movements together as proved possible in support of a common objective, to obtain an enquiry into the workings of the economic and monetary system.

To this end a petition was drafted, addressed to His Majesty the King in the following terms:

A Petition concerning the ABOLITION OF POVERTY, and the Removal of the Main causes of ECONOMIC WARFARE between the Nations.

TO THE KING'S MOST EXCELLENT MAJESTY.

The PETITION of Your Majesty's loyal subjects whose names are appended hereto showeth that:

21

1. **Whereas** great numbers of your subjects in divers wide areas are in the extremity of want, for the relief of which the capital and money-incomes of all classes of your subjects are heavily taxed,
   NEVERTHELESS food and goods in great quantities have been and are continuing to be destroyed;

2. **Whereas** great numbers of your subjects have been for many years deprived of gainful occupation, in default whereof all classes of your subjects are heavily taxed to maintain their fellow citizens,
   NEVERTHELESS work on the production of food and goods has been and is still being deliberately restricted;

3. **Whereas** Invention and Scientific Method have released great new resources of wealth,
   NEVERTHELESS the Realm as yet lacks the new principle demanded by the changed circumstances for the utilisation of such wealth;

4. **Whereas** your subjects are desirous of living at peace with the peoples of other countries, engaging with them in a natural interchange of goods and services,
   NEVERTHELESS exporters and importers are subject to great restriction of trade to the jeopardy of international amity;

We therefore, referring particularly to the fact that these circumstances are without parallel or precedent in the history of this Realm, do humbly pray **Your Most Excellent Majesty** that in exercise of **Your Royal Prerogative** you summon such and so many of your **Judges** as you deem advisable, to inquire into the circumstances above referred to, with particular reference to the following questions:

1. Whether such destruction of goods and restriction of production be not contrary to Public Policy;

2. Whether the PURPOSE of an economic and financial system ought to be the utilisation of the full products of Agriculture and Industry, so as to meet the needs of all classes in the Realm so far as possible, without respect unto persons;

3. Whether, and what amendments ought to be introduced into the economic and monetary system to the end that the rights and obligations of your subjects may be defined with

regard to the novel effects of Invention and Scientific
Method, and to the end that poverty may be abolished and
taxation reduced, and also to the end that one of the main
causes of economic warfare between the nations may be
removed so far as lies in the power of this Realm and a
beneficent example set to the whole of mankind;

And that you direct that there be called and heard in person
for all the purposes of the Inquiry those responsible persons and
representatives of organisations who claim that such amendments are possible

And that all facts be brought into consideration which the
testimony of such persons and representatives shows to be relevant to the Inquiry

And that the findings of your **Judges** be presented before the
Lords and Commons so as to be implemented by legislation
and if necessary expedited by **Orders in Council**

All which we most humbly pray of **Your Most Excellent
Majesty**, as springing from the right and liberty of your subjects
freely to enjoy those material benefits and that economic
security to which the nature and extent of the natural resources
and productive capacity of the Realm entitle them.

A Petition Council, representative of the organisations
which were co-operating in the campaign, was formed as a co-
ordinating body. Although virtually ignored by the national
press, the Petition movement spread all over the country and
also in the Dominions, particularly in New Zealand, where a
large number of signatures were obtained. These were brought
to the United Kingdom by Major General Sir Andrew Russell.
Although this activity received very little notice in the press it
was something of a surprise when the *Morning Post* even
refused to take an advertisement. This asked for loyal British
citizens who were concerned to see poverty abolished and the
removal of the causes of war to link up with the Petition movement, but the advertisement was refused for what seemed very
flimsy reasons.

The Petition campaign was greatly helped by the Christian
churches of all denominations. In particular, the Roman
Catholics were very supportive. Many of the Catholic Bishops
were signatories to the petition and gave active support. They

were greatly influenced by the statement by Pope Pius XI in *Quadragessimo Anno 106–9*:

> It has been obvious that in our day wealth and immense power have been concentrated in the hands of a few men . . . This power becomes particularly irresistible when exercised by those who, because they hold and control money, are also able to control to whom it should be allotted. In that, they supply the life-blood, so to speak, of the whole economic body. They have their grasp on the very soul of production, so that no-one dare breathe against their will.

It was also a privilege to meet the late Dr William Temple, Archbishop of Canterbury, who was very forthright on the subject. He wrote in his book *The Hope of a New World*:

> It cannot be justified in modern conditions that the Banks should, in order to meet national needs, create credit which earns interest for themselves. The State must resume the right to control and issue and cancellation of every kind of money. Till that is done, a body within the community will control what is vital to the community, and that is a false principle.

As a result I found myself holding forth from the pulpit of Christ Church, Westminster, at the invitation of the Rev. P. T. R. Kirk of the Industrial Christian Fellowship, and reading the lesson at the Whitfield's Tabernacle at the invitation of the Rev. Albert Belden.

As Honorary Secretary of the Petition movement I became increasingly aware that we needed larger premises. We were operating in two small offices in Sentinel House, Southampton Row. We were, of course, very short of money to organise a national campaign, but we were fortunate in being able to take on the end of a lease in Grosvenor Place, near Victoria, at a rent we could just afford. This enabled us to form a Petition Club and to house this and the offices in a really central position. A number of our supporters, including Vincent Vickers, formerly a director of the Bank of England, Lord Northbourne, who became the first President of the Club, Sir Reginald Rowe, assistant treasurer of Lincoln's Inn, Sir Alliot Verdon-Roe, the air pioneer, and others agreed to become guarantors. The Club opened in 1936 with a reception attended by about 200 people.

Although I was still working full-time in overseas communications I succeeded in getting two months' leave without pay to organise the furnishing and other arrangements connected with this development.

I still recall the excitement of this period. Funds at our disposal were totally inadequate, yet we went ahead to furnish a four-storey house as Club premises. We did this by going to the many sales of furniture and other effects which took place in the Whitfield Street area, behind Tottenham Court Road. Thus we bought settees for ten shillings, armchairs for a similar amount, a set of dining-room chairs for twenty-five shillings, a library table for twelve shillings and sixpence and many similar items at prices which even then were absurd.

Though obviously not in the best of condition, when re-covered they proved eminently satisfactory and lasted for many years. We also had gifts of furniture, notably from Lady Wolsey, who sent us a mixed bag she had held in store. This proved something of an embarrassment, for a great deal of it was cane furniture full of wood-worm. It was with the greatest difficulty that we finally persuaded Lady Wolsey to allow us to dispose of it.

We all felt that we were making real progress. Branch Petition groups were being formed all over the country and signatures were flowing in. We were undoubtedly helped by the accession of Edward VIII to the throne. Many people thought he would be sympathetic to the ideas in the Petition particularly in view of his declaration that 'something must be done', which he made when he visited the South Wales coal fields and saw the state of the miners and their families.

The organisation of the Petition movement was also helped by linking up with John Park who, together with W. J. Brown, a former Labour MP, had formed a Younger Generations movement. This was also centred at our Grosvenor Place headquarters. The main burden of organising the Club and the movement in the early days fell largely on John Park and myself, ably assisted by a young and enthusiastic secretary, Miss Cecilia Hodson.

Unfortunately, however, it was not all plain sailing. Some of

our most important supporters, including the President, Lord
Northbourne, were persuaded that the growth of the movement
necessitated the appointment of a full-time organiser. In due
course a Major Orr-Ewing was appointed and a fund was raised
to enable him to take over the task. We naturally presumed that
he would work with us and operate from our Grosvenor Place
headquarters, but when John Park and I returned from Ipswich,
where we had visited a Petition shop which had just been set up,
we found that the offices had been moved to Victoria Street.

Needless to say, this came as a blow. The Club had been
formed specifically to provide a centre for the Petition movement; without it there did not seem much purpose in carrying
on. After a time, we began to realise that the Club had
developed a life of its own. It was re-named the Economic
Reform Club, and we began to reorganise our aims and objectives in the light of the new developments.

In the meantime, the Petition movement itself began to slow
down. The abdication of Edward VIII dealt it a blow which,
together with the rather dictatorial methods adopted by the new
organiser, proved fatal.

In October, 1938, some 69,000 signatures were presented
by the Mayor of Coventry, on behalf of 60,000 Coventry people.
A procession was organised by Robert Scrutton, supported by
clergy of all denominations, the British Legion, Toc H and
many other organisations. The outbreak of war prevented
further presentations being made, though there were many
thousands more signatures which had been collected during the
campaign. These were stored in the vaults of a bank in the
Strand throughout the war and afterwards we had reluctantly to
decide that they should be destroyed as they were no longer
valid. So ended a valiant effort to remove the causes of poverty
and war!

So far as the Petition Movement was concerned, all the funds
provided had been used up and the Petition, which had seemed
to hold out such promise, faded into insignificance.

On the other hand, the Economic Reform Club gained in
membership and influence, and although we had to give up our
house in Grosvenor Place there was sufficient support to move
to even more suitable premises in Great Cumberland Place,
near Marble Arch.

As the activities of the Club increased, so did the membership, and it was decided to add 'and Institute' to our title, as it was felt that the wider interests of the members merited this addition. The house in Great Cumberland Place proved a great success, but once again we were doomed to disappointment. The house had been leased from a doctor who unfortunately went bankrupt. Efforts to take over the head-lease proved abortive, so once again we had to look around for new premises. Fortunately, a house in Grosvenor Place, a few doors from our original address, became available and we moved once again.

We set about establishing even more adequate club premises, with a snack bar and one or two bedrooms for members. This was all done on a shoestring, but somehow just enough funds were available to make it all possible. I still managed to direct the affairs of the Club on a voluntary basis, dividing my time between these activities and earning a living.

One of the outstanding meetings held in the Club in 1939 was the talk given by Compton Mackenzie, when he spoke on the subject of the economic aspects of the Abdication. Needless to say, the Club was packed to the doors for this occasion.

We arranged many interesting meetings in those pre-war years, one of the most important being the dinner we organised at the Savoy Hotel in honour of Sir John (later Lord) Boyd Orr. I well remember meeting him at his club when I put the suggestion to him that we wanted to arrange such a function. He welcomed the idea, and we set about bringing together a dinner committee to sponsor the project. Everyone we approached, including peers and MPs of all parties, agreed to serve, and we assembled a really significant group to support the event. Among those who agreed to join was Ernest Bevin, then an up-and coming trade union leader, Vernon Bartlett, an Independent MP, W. Craven-Ellis, MP, Viscount Bledisloe, The Earl of Feversham, Sir Ernest Graham-Little, MP, Lord Horder, Dr Julian Huxley, P. C. Loftus, MP, Viscount Lymington, Compton Mackenzie, Lord Meston, Lord Northbourne, The Earl of Oxford and Asquith, Sir Reginald Rowe, Lord Sempill and Professor Soddy.

The subject of Sir John's address was 'Health, Agriculture and the Standard of Living'. Vincent Vickers took the Chair,

supported by Lord Sempill and Lord Horder, and the 350
guests, who represented many groups and interests in the country,
gave the speech an enthusiastic reception.

In spite of our efforts to enlist the support of the national press,
very little publicity was given to what we thought was an
important contribution. We had entertained representatives of
all the leading papers at the dinner and in addition had made
personal approaches to some editors. For example, I invited
Frank Owen, then editor of the *Evening Standard*, whom I
knew personally, to have lunch with me especially to tell him of
the event and to seek his support. On the following day the
Standard devoted its front page to the comments of some
relatively unknown person, and there was no mention of Sir
John's speech. This was also typical of the daily press.

All went well with the Club until the outbreak of war in 1939.
For a time, for the period of the 'phoney' war, things went on
much as before. One event which made a distinct impression on
me was a visit by the Duke of Bedford soon after war broke out.
We employed a somewhat dim maid who came into my room
with the information that a man was at the door wanting to see
me. On going to the front door I found the Duke patiently waiting on the doorstep. He had arrived in his brougham with two
outriders and it seemed a most discourteous reception, to say
the least!

However, I immediately took him inside and he then told me
that he wished to acquaint some of those whose views he valued
of the steps he and John McGovern, MP, had taken to try to
bring hostilities to an end. He presented me with a list of provisions which he claimed had been agreed by Hitler. These
were certainly very far-reaching and, if genuine, could, in my
view, have made it possible to reach an agreement on the ces-
sation of hostilities. But, and it is a very big but, were they
genuine? Certainly Lord Halifax and the Government did not
believe them and the project fizzled out. Some time after this
the Duke retired to his estate in Scotland.

He told me that a detective visited him every afternoon to
ensure that he stayed put and he expected to be arrested under
18B at any moment. Certainly Herbert Morrison wanted to do
this, but it is said that Winston Churchill would not allow it to
be carried out.

Although the Duke of Bedford gave the impression of being rather cold and unapproachable, it is certain that it was not his intention. He had readily accepted the invitation to become President of the original Prosperity League which we founded in the early days, he also became a Vice-President of the Economic Reform Club when it was founded in 1936, but his pacifist outlook during the war caused many members to call for his resignation. I had the difficult and distasteful task of writing to him to convey this view, which I did not relish as I had known him for many years and appreciated the sincerity of his views. However, his reply was typical, he merely accepted the situation without any hard feeling and he confirmed his support in our efforts to reform the monetary system although he was no longer a member.

One amusing story about him was told me by Morley Tonkin, his ward. Lord Tavistock, as he then was, attended a week-end conference in Hertfordshire, and it was decided by some of those present at the conference to play a joke on him. He always wore a peak cap with a little button on the top. During the week-end this was purloined and on the last night of the conference a torch-light procession was formed and the cap was ceremoniously buried in the grounds. The next morning, Lord Tavistock, together with others who had attended the conference, travelled by rail to London and of course Lord T was bareheaded, but not a word was said. On arrival at Liverpool Street everyone watched to see what would happen. They were rewarded when Lord T marched into Dunn's, the hatters, and emerged a few minutes later wearing precisely the same kind of cap as had been ceremoniously buried the previous night.

The Night that I Guarded the Bank of England!

On the outbreak of war in 1939 an incident occurred which had little or no bearing on economic reform, but is perhaps worth telling. For some years I had been a member of the City of London Police Reserve and was called up to Moor Lane police station to take a spell of duty. This was in response to the threat of Irish terrorists, who had become active with a campaign of planting bombs. As it happened, by the time I reported for duty, war had been declared and London was completely blacked out.

On reporting at Moor Lane police station I was told that my beat was round the Bank of England and adjacent streets. As one of the many critics of Montagu Norman and his Court of Directors of the Bank, I found some amusement in the fact that I had this particular beat. However, I set off for the Bank and began my patrol. It was soon dark, and in the black-out, with no moon, one had almost to feel one's way around. As I patrolled my thoughts turned to the strange enigmatic figure who controlled the Bank and its affairs, The Right Hon. Montagu Norman, DSO, alias Professor Clarence Skinner, who had been the evil genius in persuading the government of the day to return to the gold standard in 1925. So much that had gone wrong in Britain's economy—the unemployment, malnutrition, bankruptcies—could all be laid to the door of this man and his supporters in the financial world.

I recalled Winston Churchill's condemnation of the experts who had persuaded him, as Chancellor of the Exchequer, to return to gold and his speech in the House of Commons in which he said how wrong was this decision. I also recalled what my friend, Vincent Vickers, had told me of the day he had told Montagu Norman that he would fight his policies to the end. I also thought of the strange link between Governor Norman with Dr Schacht, adviser to Adolf Hitler, and the reports I had read of the international financial controls exercised by the financial hierarchy. All these thoughts and Montagu Norman's famous remark at the Mansion House dinner in 1933 when, referring to his critics, he said 'The dogs may bark, but the caravan marches on'.

After a couple of hours, my tin hat weighing a ton, I was becoming a bit bored patrolling empty streets, a very occasional bus appearing with dimmed lights giving the only sign of life. As I came to the public convenience just over the road from the Bank I heard a cockney voice calling out 'Say, Guv, are you a copper?'. I crossed the road and found the attendant waiting at the top of the steps. 'Yes,' I said, 'I am a sort of copper. What's the trouble?' 'Well,' he said, 'a bloke just came into the convenience and he had a brown paper parcel under his arm. We've been warned about bomb outrages and when I watched him go out he no longer had the parcel.' 'What do you want me to do?' I queried. 'Come down and look into all the cubicles to see if he left it somewhere.'

I must say I did not fancy this, but realising that I was the only representative of the law available, I waited until the chap patrolling the next beat appeared out of the dark and then explained the position to him. 'Tell them I died doing my duty,' I told him as I descended the stairs. My impression is that the attendant and I examined about 20 cubicles without any result. And then, there was a brown paper parcel tucked up behind the water pipe under the cistern. Taking a deep breath, I reached up for the parcel and held it gingerly, listening all the time for the dreaded ticking sound. But it was completely silent. Somewhat relieved, I told the attendant to fetch a bucket of water, not knowing if this was the correct procedure. 'You sure it's safe?' asked the attendant. 'Yes' I said, carefully lowering the package into the bucket of water.

What to do now, I wondered. I told the attendant to find a stick and began to probe the package very gently. Nothing happened, so I began to prod more vigorously and at last succeeded in undoing it. Out came a ham roll, a piece of cake and various other similar items.

We both breathed a sigh of relief, and I went back to my lonely patrol feeling that I had really guarded the Bank of England and could resume my criticisms of its policies.

The Club continued to function at 26 Grosvenor Place until, one Sunday afternoon, a German plane came down near Victoria Station and badly damaged the house. I had been on duty in the City that afternoon, and when I went along to see the damage I realised that we could no longer continue to use the premises. So we had, once again, to seek new premises, and in the light of the increased bombing raids we decided to move to a less vulnerable part of London. As I was still living in the Muswell Hill area a house was found which was large enough for us and one of our sub-tenants. Having established ourselves in the new house, the very same night a bomb fell and demolished a house a few doors away. Our roof was badly holed, it poured with rain and I have vivid memories of carting our valuable stores of books and duplicating paper which had been moved to the top floor down three flights of stairs. It was a hectic night.

The following circular was sent to members of the Economic

Reform Club on the 19th October 1940, which reflects the circumstances of those days. It is, perhaps, worth reproducing:

Bulletins & Bombs

Once again we have to apologise for the non-appearance of the October Bulletin. We had fully intended to issue this on the 15th of the month, but fate, in the shape of a high explosive bomb, which inconsiderately fell a few yards away from our new premises just as we were getting straight has made any attempt at producing a bulletin out of the question.

Our new house was proving very convenient, and we had been able to get ourselves reasonably well established, when at 1.30 in the morning the trouble occurred. Practically all the windows in the front of the house were blown out, large chunks of stones and debris were distributed throughout the house, and most of the top floor ceiling deposited itself on the floors. Tiles and slates were broken, we spent our time running round with buckets and pails, trying to save precious literature and duplicating paper from damage by the heavy rain.

All this has not been conducive to progress towards economic reform, but tribute must be paid to the gallant staff who, under impossible conditions, have continued to deal with correspondence, send out orders and generally keep things going.

The normal disorganisation caused by removing the considerable amount of furniture and other effects, to say nothing of the paper, books etc. with frequent air raid warnings intervening had been bad enough, but words fail to describe the result of this together with a visitation like the one we have just experienced.

However, we are determined to carry on, believing that our work is truly worth-while, and required more than ever.

4

ECONOMIC TRIBULATION

An illustration of the value to the community of a small but well-informed and determined group of people was given on the outbreak of war in 1939, when, in line with orthodox financial technique, bank rate was automatically doubled. This would have meant that the interest paid by Government in its need to borrow from the banking system to finance the war effort would have risen to astronomic proportions, as it did in 1914–18. Led by Mr Craven Ellis, MP, a group of MPs of all parties put pressure on the Government and the Bank of England to reduce bank rate. Supported by Sir Charles Morgan-Webb and other members of the Economic Reform Club, we succeeded in getting the bank rate brought down, and thus saved the country a vast sum in interest charges which would have been automatically imposed if orthodox views had prevailed.

Some of us in the Economic Reform Club wanted to take the question further. The following is an extract from a letter sent to Sir John Simon, Chancellor of the Exchequer, on 13 February 1940. In it, we argued

> that creation of such additional money and credit as may be necessary for the prosecution of the war should be the function of the State and that the Banking System should be called upon to act in this matter as the Agents of Government and not as the lenders of money. It appears to my Committee that this is a fundamental issue and that no satisfactory solution of our financial problem will be found until the Government in the above mentioned circumstances ceases either directly or indirectly to play the role of borrowers and to put upon the nation a consequent burden of debt without any such justification as exists when money is borrowed from genuine savings. There is not in the creation of such additional money any question of savings and there ought not, we suggest, to be any question of lending.

It is hoped that you will see your way to make some definite pronouncement on this matter as there is a growing feeling of concern that the Government are placing themselves and the nation as a whole in a false position by continuing to allow private institutions to usurp the functions which rightly belong to the State and in doing so to place upon the community a burden which they ought not to be called upon to bear.

While we were successful in our efforts to reduce the cost of Government wartime borrowing, our challenge on the more controversial issue failed to impress the authorities.

In 1939 I lost a very good friend when Vincent Vickers died. He was an outstanding character, and some years later his cousin, Antony Vickers, asked me to write an appreciation of V. C. V. from which the following extracts are taken:

The father of all economists, Adam Smith, wrote, 'It is not from the benevolence of the butcher, the brewer, or the baker, that we expect our dinner, but from their regard of their own interests. We address ourselves, not to their humanity, but to their self-love.' That this is true of the majority of mankind few will deny, yet there has always been a tiny minority of people, from all walks of life, who have deliberately put self-interest on one side for the sake of a cause in which they truly believe.

One outstanding character was certainly Vincent Cartwright Vickers. He was outstanding for two main reasons; firstly for his complete sincerity and honesty, and secondly for his disregard for personal aggrandizement. In his latter years his convictions drove him to take a course completely at variance with his own self-interest, yet he did this in such a disarming way that few were conscious of the very real sacrifices of wealth and health he was prepared to make for the cause in which he believed.

This was allied to a lively sense of humour, which enabled him to debunk so much of the hypocrisy which abounded in the 'good old days'. He was one of those fortunate people who inherited considerable wealth, in modern parlance 'a bloated capitalist'. Nine-tenths of his income came from investments, and in his day this gave him position and all those things to

which most men aspire in a lifetime of hard work. He had all
these things without effort, yet he dedicated himself to a cause
which could only bring him opprobrium and even hostility from
those with whom he was associated in the world of finance.

Vincent Vickers was born on January 16th, 1879, by which
time the firm which bore his name had become a great power in
the country. The demand for steel had grown rapidly in the
nineteenth century, and the industry was expanding tremen-
dously with all the demands being made in building railways,
ships, bridges, and the vast developments of the first Industrial
Revolution. The Sheffield firm of Vickers had prospered and
grown enormously, and the name became a household word the
world over.

He went to Eton and then to Magdalen College, Oxford, and
in the course of time became a Director of Vickers, an appointment he held for twenty-two years. In 1910 he was invited to
become a Director of the Bank of England. With characteristic
modesty he always said of this appointment that it arose
because he represented heavy industry, was about the right age,
with the right kind of background, and at the same time knew
nothing at all about financial policy. This, he said, was an
obvious reason for making him a Director of the Bank of
England. He often told me of his experiences when he attended
meetings of the Court of Directors.

Montagu Norman was then Governor, and with other
knowledgeable merchant bankers he formed a caucus who were
able, with their intimate knowledge of the business of banking
and finance, to ensure their policies were accepted by other
members of the Court without very much trouble.

It was not for some years that Vincent Vickers began to query
whether these policies were in the best interests of the country.
He was very concerned with business affairs, he had many
interests and being Director of the Bank of England carried
considerable prestige, including being made a Deputy Lieutenant
of the City of London. It was when he fell desperately ill and
during the period when he was slowly recuperating that he
began to use his critical faculties to re-examine the policies he
had until then accepted without too much query.

The period of isolation from the pressing world of affairs provided an opportunity which he had so far lacked, and this enabled him to think out the effects on the country and its people of the rigid financial policies maintained by Montagu Norman. This period of analysis of economic and financial policies accepted by most politicians, industrialists, and others almost without question led him to the conclusion that the operation of this system had been a disaster. He resigned from the Bank of England in 1919, but it was not until the crucial decision to return to the gold standard of 1925 that his conscience drove him actively to oppose the policies of Montagu Norman and the Government of the day.

Of this decision he subsequently wrote:

> Ever since that day in 1926, when not in arrogance but with humility I felt it my duty to explain to the Governor of the Bank of England that henceforth I was going to fight him and the gold standard and the Bank of England policy until I died, I have been an ardent money reformer, since when I have spent much time and money in advocating the necessity for a reform of the monetary system.

The Chancellor of the Exchequer responsible for carrying out the policy of the Bank of England was Winston Churchill. Perhaps the best tribute that could be paid to the correctness of the views of Vincent Vickers in his courageous head-on collision with the policies of Montagu Norman in 1926 was contained in the forthright condemnation by Winston Churchill of the decision to return to the gold standard made in the Budget debate in the House of Commons on April 21st, 1932 [to which reference was made in Chapter 2].

There could be no clearer vindication of the views which V. C. V. placed before Montagu Norman in 1926, yet the main case which he put forward in the 1930s is still not accepted years later by the economic and financial pundits: that is, the need for an honest money system. As he puts it, 'We do not possess and have never possessed, a true and honest measure of value.' Although the orthodoxy of today is different from the orthodoxy of the 1930s the monetary system still remains unsatisfactory, and the words V. C. V. wrote in 1939 are as true today as they were then: 'I believe that the existing system is actively harmful to the State, creates poverty and unemployment, and is the root cause of war.'

The last fifteen years of his life were spent, with other like-minded men and women, in a single-minded attempt to arouse his fellow-countrymen to the immense dangers inherent in an unsound monetary policy, and he based his case on his own very wide experience and knowledge gained from his years in industry and the Bank of England. This meant resigning from many of his directorships, including the family firm of Vickers Ltd, and it also meant that to many of his contemporaries he was labelled as a crank, with all that this implies in orthodox and respectable circles!

It is an interesting speculation to consider how very different would be the position of Britain today had his warning given in 1926 been heeded by the authorities. Looking back to the immense harm done to industry, to the well-being of millions of British people, to the unemployment with its accompanying degradation, to the malnutrition and poverty, to the destruction of good labour relations, it is surely obvious that had the suffering and misery brought about by the policy of deflation been avoided, the outlook and position of our country today could have been revolutionised.

There is no doubt that the trail of bitterness and frustration brought about by the existence of very nearly three million unemployed in 1930 could have been avoided, and today we are reaping the whirlwind in resistance to change, restrictive practices, go-slows, strikes and other manifestations of irrational behaviour. The memory of the traumatic experience of the 1930s, when men, women and children went hungry while we burned crops, poured milk down drains, and ruined many large and small enterprises, is largely responsible for much that goes wrong in human relations to this day.

V. C. V.'s appeal was to common sense; he urged that the right course was to combine Christian principles with practical business abilities. He had a keen sense of humour, and the ability to tell a story which cannot be conveyed by the printed word. He was a born raconteur, and one of his favourite stories concerned the Bank of England.

It was after he had resigned his Directorship and Britain had returned to a modified form of gold standard. Under these provisions holders of £2500 in notes were entitled to change them for an equivalent amount in gold specie. So one day he packed £2500 in notes in a briefcase and went along to the Bank of England to ask for a bar of gold. The clerk behind the counter was visibly worried by this unusual request; he had no knowledge of any such provision. After much consultation with higher authority he at last agreed that the transaction was in order, and the bar of gold was duly brought up from the vaults of the bank. As he carefully wrapped this up in a piece of brown paper to hand to this unusual client, the clerk said, 'Excuse me, Sir, but there has been much interest aroused in the bank by your request. Could you tell me why you want a bar of gold?' To which V. C. V. replied 'I want to use it as a door-stop!'

Vincent Vickers died on November 3rd, 1939 after a long illness which sapped his physical strength. Yet he went on with his attempt to write and to put on record his convictions until the day he died. A few days before his death he wrote to me: 'My keen desire to help up to the end has been the sole incentive which has enabled me to carry on perhaps a few weeks longer.' Twelve months after his death I was asked to go to an office in the City, and there I was handed a parcel containing a mass of papers which comprised all the notes, memoranda and other writings which he had requested should be collected and handed to me after his death.

Much of the material was incomplete, and in his own handwriting, which was not always a model of clarity. After struggling with this mass of material for some time, and realising that in wartime conditions I had little hope of doing very much about it, I sent it to his eldest daughter, Lady Cawdor. She wrote to me rather despairingly about it, but then suddenly she found it possible to put it all together in book form, and this was subsequently published by the Bodley Head under the title *Economic Tribulation*. It has been reprinted in the United States, Australia and New Zealand and has had a remarkable circulation all over the world.

Other policies have prevailed in the years since V. C. V. died; no-one can claim that these have produced satisfactory results, either to Britain, or in other countries. The inspiration of the last years of Vincent Vickers' life lives on, and there are many who are carrying on in the spirit of the opening words of *Economic Tribulation*: 'In so far as we are able, we must try to assist our fellow-men to understand. This we can do fearlessly, for that which is mistaken or false will carry no weight and will be lost and forgotten, whilst that which is true will prevail.' (*This appreciation was written in 1969.*)

5

WARTIME
DEVELOPMENTS

Progress made under war conditions was quite surprising. A
lively interest grew in economic affairs, particularly in the forces.
By the time the war ended the Club had established a membership of nearly 2000 and had no less than ten provincial
branches in Birmingham, Leeds, Chesterfield, Sheffield,
Nottingham, Liverpool, Leicester, Heckmondwike, Edinburgh
and Brighton. We also spread overseas, establishing branches
in Australia, New Zealand, Kenya, Southern Rhodesia and
South Africa.

In 1942 we published an important booklet entitled *A Twentieth Century Economic System*. The author, who at that time
wished to remain anonymous, was A. de V. Leigh, Secretary of
the London Chamber of Commerce, who had made a special
study of problems arising in international trade. He put forward
a plan for a system of international trade and payments which is
still relevant today. *The Times* devoted a whole column to a
summary of the proposals and the booklet achieved a
worldwide circulation. I was to base a broadcast talk on this
theme in 1947, to which reference will be made later.

An activity which also resulted in a great deal of publicity
was a conference arranged in London with the title 'The World
We Want'. This took place in 1942 and was organised jointly
by the Economic Reform Club and the Industrial Christian
Fellowship. The terms of reference were:

> To discuss practical proposals for the future guidance of British
> Policy and that of the British Commonwealth of Nations so that
> after this war we may take our full share in banishing the twin evils
> of Fear and Want.

Very little was being done officially at this time to look at the
post-war scene, yet there was a widespread desire on the part of

all sections of the community for some lead towards a better society. We had a number of eminent contributors, including Sir Richard Gregory, Robert Boothby, MP, Sir John Boyd Orr, MP, P. C. Loftus, MP, Lord Portsmouth, Sir Reginald Rowe, Lord Sempill, Sir George Stapleton and Norman Mansbridge, the founder of the Workers Educational Association. The plans they put forward were met with approval by an audience of some 250 people from all over the country and the speeches were given valuable press coverage.

An interesting personal development occurred during the weekend while I was fully engaged with the 'World We Want' conference. It was at the same time as the Annual Meeting of the Association of Scientific Workers, and I had been largely responsible for the recent formation of a branch of this Association in Cable and Wireless and had been made Chairman of the branch. The AScW had only recently become a Trade Union and at the time we were their largest branch. Although I could not be present I was voted on to the National Executive and I remained a member of this for twelve months. It was a strange experience and I did not find it very rewarding, for I had little in common with my fellow members on the Executive, who were, not surprisingly, far to the left of me.

It was the combination of this activity and my fulltime occupation with Cable and Wireless, coupled with the rapid growth of the Economic Reform Club with all that this entailed in increasing work-load, that caused me to be physically and mentally exhausted.

At this time I had a very strange experience. I was going on night duty at 5 p.m. in the afternoon and, confronted with 14 hours' of concentrated effort, I felt that it would be impossible to see the night through. I collapsed on the bus seat and thought 'Oh God, how can I manage to work all night?', and as I thought this, an immense flow of energy seemed to pour right through me, from the top of my spine to my fingers and toes. The amazing thing was that this injection of energy carried me through the night without any difficulty. I have never forgotten this sudden source of energy which transformed me from a feeling of intense fatigue to ability to work normally for 14 hours of concentrated effort.

However, working all night at Electra House, the head-quarters of Cable and Wireless, and dealing with the activities arising from the Economic Reform Club during the day, thus getting very little sleep and not very adequate meals, eventually proved too much. Added to this was anxiety caused by the fact that I was ordered to go overseas by Cable and Wireless.

In spite of an appeal to Sir Edward Wilshaw, Chairman of Cable and Wireless, signed by twelve peers and MPs of all parties, urging that the work I was doing in the economic sphere was of such importance in the national interest that I should be allowed to remain in the UK, the order to go overseas was confirmed. This appeal was signed by members of both Houses and all parties, including the Earl of Portsmouth, Lord Northbourne, Lord Sempill, Sir Reginald Rowe, R. R. Stokes, MP, W. J. Brown, MP, Andrew MacLaren, MP, Clement Davies, MP, P. C. Loftus, MP and W. Craven-Ellis, MP.

The result of overwork and anxiety finally caused a break-down, and my doctor confronted me with a choice—either give up the voluntary work I was doing in the economic sphere or resign my career with Cable and Wireless.

I had no hesitation in deciding on the latter course. Looking back over the 40-odd years which have elapsed since I made this rather bold decision, I have no reason to regret it. Although I was entitled to a pension, as I resigned due to ill-health, my application was refused. I did not pursue this: my break with overseas communication was complete.

For some time I had to take things rather quietly, but the intense relief at being released from the pressure of working at night and coping with my main interest during the day helped restore me, and I was now able to devote my time and effort to the interests which had increasingly absorbed my life.

We had, among members of the Economic Reform Club, a number of industrialists and professional people who were keen to play a part in the campaign for economic reform. Some of them came together to form a Research Committee, under the Chairmanship of Lawrence Jackson, a very able civil servant, and a number of useful pamphlets and other papers were produced. We met on a Saturday at the Farmer's Club in London once a month, and devoted a whole day to our deliberations.

This continued throughout the war and for several years after. Among the wartime publications was a series of pamphlets entitled 'The Banks and the War'. It ran to five papers, and the first gave details of correspondence with the Chancellor of the Exchequer, to which reference has already been made (page 00).

The second of the pamphlets dealt with statements made by the Joint Stock Banks, and reiterated our view that there was no justification for the Government continuing a policy of 'borrowing' the nation's credit from the banks and paying interest thereon.

The third gave details of our correspondence with Sir Kingsley Wood, then Chancellor of the Exchequer. Needless to say, we got little change from the Treasury, but a number of MPs raised questions in the House along the same lines as our submissions. These included R. R. Stokes, P. C. Loftus, W. Craven-Ellis, Ruper de la Bere and others. The following text of a letter sent to Sir Kingsley Wood in January 1943 summarises our case:

To the Right Honourable, Sir Kingsley Wood, MP,
Chancellor of the Exchequer.

January 12, 1943.

Dear Sir,

I am directed by the Research Committee of the Economic Reform Club to refer to your letter of December 9 and to express both disappointment and concern that the representations made by them should be dismissed on such grounds as are given in the statements made by you in the House of Commons referred to in your letter. In the view of the Committee these statements are not only inconclusive, but appear to indicate a perplexing degree of reticence in dealing with such matters.

This, we think, is regrettable, as there is a large and growing number of people who wish to be fully informed and who are prepared to give full support to a policy which can be shown to mobilise to the best advantage the whole of the financial resources of the nation in support of the war effort. It appears to the Committee that although you have assumed control over the operations of the Banks you are still content to allow them to monetise the nation's credit and treat it as their own. The Committee again wish to point out that, in creating credit for the purpose of bridging the gap between the income and expenditure of the Government, the Banks are not utilising their own financial resources and there is no justification for treating such credit creations as if they were genuine savings.

The recent pamphlet, *What is Banking?*, by the Right Honourable Reginald McKenna, does not in the least invalidate this statement; indeed it strongly supports it. In effect Mr McKenna states that the ability of the Joint Stock Banks to 'lend' to the Government depends upon the operations of the Bank of England in increasing bank cash, and that these operations in turn are now controlled by the Government. To put the matter more bluntly, it can be stated that the Joint Stock Banks, generally speaking, can only increase their loans to the Government if the Government itself provides them (through the Bank of England) with increased bank cash, when they can not only proceed to 'lend' this increase to the Government, but multiply such 'loans' up to ten times the increase. Surely this is a Gilbertian situation.

My Committee wish me to take this opportunity of referring to answers given by you in the House of Commons to Mr Craven-Ellis, MP, dealing with the Fiduciary Issue of October 22 and November 26, and to state that here again it is difficult to understand why reticence should be shown in your answers. We suggest that it is in the public interest that the public should know what sum or sums they have to pay for the management of the Fiduciary Issue.

In short, we feel that the public is being kept in ignorance on financial matters, and it is not being given a square deal to which it is entitled by reason of its efforts in the prosecution of the war and its anxiety to maintain stability of the currency, so far as may be possible, both now and during the period of reconstruction.

Yours faithfully,
Edward Holloway,
Hon. Secretary.

Obviously the publication of this series and the number of Parliamentary Questions arising therefrom aroused the concern of the banks, who were very conscious of the widespread interest which had sprung from this activity. Not only were questions asked in the British House of Commons, but also in overseas legislatures. MPs in Canada, Australia and New Zealand had taken up the challenge. The Honourable Wright Patman had made in a speech in the US House of Representatives, giving support to our submissions, a copy of which was appended to the Congressional Record for 16 December, 1942.

Thus we were emboldened to produce No. 4 in the series. In this we took to task Mr Reginald McKenna, Chairman of the Midland Bank, whose pamphlet *What is Banking?* had been published in an obvious attempt to counter our campaign. Sir Reginald Rowe wrote:

> Mr McKenna's last effort *What is Banking?* was in the nature of a *Volte Face*. In his old age he seems to have grown nervous of the effects of theories which not so long ago he bravely championed.

The final pamphlet of the series was a record of correspondence between the President of the Institute of Bankers in Scotland, Mr J. Mackenzie, and our Research Committee. Mr Mackenzie challenged our view on the creation of money and described our activities as 'misdirected, misconceived and mischievous'. He claimed that 'It is not the Banks but the borrower—any borrower—who "creates" credit'. It took over 30 years to establish the facts about the creation of credit, when the true state of affairs was established beyond any doubt by the evidence submitted to the Radcliffe Committee on Credit and Currency in 1959.

In 1944 we succeeded in setting up an all-Party Parliamentary Committee with Robert Boothby as Chairman, P. C. Loftus as Secretary and myself as organising secretary. The major preoccupation of this Committee was with the post-war plans for an international payments system. There were two major plans under consideration, the US plan by Harry Dexter White, an official of the US Treasury, and the Keynes' plan, put forward by John Maynard Keynes. We were also interested in putting forward the scheme outlined in *A Twentieth Century Economic System*, but it was the two official plans which commanded most attention.

We organised meetings all over the country in an effort to point out the dangers inherent in an international payments system which continued the pre-war debtor–creditor relationship between nations in their trading policies.

One leading politician who shared our views on this subject was Leo Amery, and we invited him to speak on 'The Commercial Conditions Attached to the Washington Loan Agreement' in April 1946. He told us:

> What I object to are the strings which have been tied to the Loan. Their object is to clamp upon the world and in particular upon the British Empire, the wholly out-of-date economic conceptions of a hundred years ago. The outlook of American industrial and political leaders today is that of the corresponding class in the England of 1846.

We sent a telegram to the Prime Minister saying 'that the meeting urges the rejection of this proposed American Loan and the Bretton Woods Agreement on the grounds that the terms are onerous, unjust and unworkable and will lead to economic disruption and the embitterment of Anglo-American relations'.

The fact that Keynes had urged that equal pressure should be brought to bear on both creditor and debtor nations to maintain equilibrium in international payments predisposed us to favour his views and to reject the White plan. In the event the Final Act of the Bretton Woods Agreement was much nearer the White plan than Keynes, and we did our best to oppose its acceptance by Parliament.

The night before the debate on the Washington Loan Agreement which, if accepted, meant that we automatically had to accept the Bretton Woods plan, Antony Vickers, with whom I worked very closely, and I arranged a dinner at the Savoy, to which MPs of all parties were invited to discuss tactics in the forthcoming debate. It was interesting that all present agreed that they would join forces to oppose the agreement, but in the event we lost the day.

It is a matter of history that the long-awaited Loan was used up in a very short time, and the USA then introduced the Marshall Plan, which was a much more enlightened approach to the problems of those days.

6

THE POST-WAR SCENE

As the war came to an end, interest in post-war development became intense and I was persuaded by Lady Rhys Williams, who had been adopted as Liberal candidate for Ilford North, to become the Liberal candidate for Ilford South. Although, at first, I was not very attracted to the idea of becoming a party politician, I did meet the local committee, and after several meetings and discussions finally decided in November 1944 that I would accept nomination. My secretary, Cecilia Hodson, agreed to become my agent and did the job remarkably well.

It was rather shattering to discover, when the election was due to take place, that all the organisation which existed in the Ilford constituency moved North, leaving the South constituency with very little. I realised that I had engaged in a somewhat forlorn hope when the Chairman of the constituency association took me for a tour of the area. As we passed a very large burial ground with masses of tombstones he pointed to these and remarked 'There are your Liberal supporters'. He was not far wrong!

The election campaign started with a large public meeting, at which Sir Herbert Samuel was the main speaker. It was supposed to be a joint meeting, covering both the North and South constituencies. However, I found myself addressing an overflow meeting, while the main speakers were holding forth to a full house in the main hall. It was only after some of my constituents protested that at the very end I was invited to join the main platform and speak for a few minutes. Some of my supporters were annoyed, and it was not a very auspicious start from my point of view.

My two opponents were James Ranger for the Labour Party and Major E. J. Boulton for the Conservatives. The campaign was fairly fought and in spite of many difficulties I enjoyed the experience immensely. Looking at some of my election material I realise that it did not owe very much to the Liberal Party, neither did I get any help from Liberal Headquarters. Several prominent Economic Reform Club supporters came to the constituency and spoke on my behalf, including Lord Sempill and Sir Charles Morgan-Webb. There was, however, little hope of winning a seat for the Liberals in the immediate post-war climate. The forces were strongly anti-Conservative and, having had a considerable degree of indoctrination from the left wing during the war period, were strongly pro-Labour. James Ranger, I think somewhat to his surprise, was elected for the South constituency and, as far as I could trace, spoke only in one debate for 20 minutes in the whole of the lifetime of the Parliament. The voting figures were: J. Ranger 19,399; E. Boulton 14,633; E. Holloway 6,322.

At least I saved my deposit, which my liberally minded bank manager had advanced to me before the campaign started. He was as relieved as I was when I was able to repay the loan.

Members of the Economic Reform Club had been very generous in subscribing to a special fund organised by Sir Tracy Gavin Jones, then President, to make it possible for me to fight the election. Without their support it would not have been possible.

After the election I decided that it would be useful to take on much more lecturing to Rotary Clubs, Round Tables and similar organisations. In fact, my first attempt at public speaking had been before the war when A. de V. Leigh asked me to deputise for him at a meeting in Swindon of the Workers' Educational Association.

A splendid character named Reuben George greeted me on arrival, and my speech was a tremendous success. The local press gave me a banner headline: 'Swindon WEA Speaker Condemns Gold Standard.' The success of this talk gave me great confidence, which led to the very considerable lecture programme I undertook after the war.

Reuben George invited me to return to Swindon on several occasions. I noticed in Dick Crossman's diaries that he too paid many visits to Swindon at the invitation of Reuben George.

In August 1945 I was given a splendid opportunity to extend my lecture programme. Returning prisoners of war were given some months for a period of rehabilitation and the RAF opened a station at Sunninghill for this purpose. I was one of their first lecturers, and went to Sunninghill on a number of occasions to lecture on post-war economics. The RAF men were a splendid audience, keen to catch up with the changes which had taken place during their enforced absence from the country.

Also in 1945 the death of Sir Reginald Rowe, who had played such a substantial part in the formation of the Club, meant that we lost a great supporter who had been with us since the Club was founded in 1936. His contribution, particularly to the affairs of the Research Committee and as Chairman, had been of enormous value. His book entitled *The Root of all Evil*, which we had published in 1940, had been widely circulated and had helped in the general educational campaign. It was only when I had the privilege of writing his obituary for *The Times* that I realised the extent of his interests, which had covered town and country planning, Sadlers Wells and the development of boys' clubs, which he had fostered and helped in addition to his work for economic reform.

With the ending of the war it became necessary to seek some more central accommodation. During the war our headquarters in Muswell Hill had served as a temporary measure, but now it seemed essential to be more in the centre of things. We therefore took the first tentative steps toward an arrangement with the Economic Research Council, of which I had been a founder-member. The Council had been founded in 1943 as the Joint Council for Economic and Monetary Research by a group representing a wide range of economic interests, under the Chairmanship of Wilfrid Hill, a Birmingham businessman who had founded the County Chemical Co. One of his famous products was Brylcreem, which he had sold to the Beecham Group at a very handsome price. There was a cruel story about Brylcreem that it was originally produced as a competitor to Min Cream, a furniture polish. When it failed in this respect, it was turned into a hair cream with splendid results! However, Wilfrid Hill was a strong supporter of economic reform, and among the founder-members he got together were Edward

Hulton, P. C. Loftus, Sir John Mactaggart, R. R. Stokes, Sir John Wardlaw-Milne, MP, Sir Reginald Rowe and myself. Although the Council started off with generous financial backing from Wilfrid Hill, it made little progress in the early days of its existence. The name was changed to Economic Research Council some time after it was formed, and a major reorganisation took place in 1946, when Sir John Mactaggart joined Wilfrid Hill in taking out a seven-year covenant.

The Council owed a great debt to Sir John, for not only did he subscribe generously to the funds, he also made available very suitable office accommodation at 55 Park Lane. He gave a great deal of his time to the affairs of the Council and was a generous host on many occasions.

Lady Rhys Williams became the Honorary Secretary and I was invited to take on a paid job as Secretary, but this did not appeal to me at the time. A full-time secretary, Mr Harold Goodwin, was then appointed, who had formerly been the press officer for the Liberal Party.

Following negotiations, we attempted to set up a mutually satisfactory arrangement between the Council and the Club whereby we made joint use of the premises at 55 Park Lane, but this proved unsatisfactory and was then discontinued.

Another short-lived adventure was the sponsoring of a new journal entitled *Rural Economy*, by the Economic Reform Club and the Rural Reconstruction Association. This was very ably edited by Jorian Jenks and continued for some time, but finally failed through lack of funds.

For some years I had written regularly to the BBC, urging that the Economic Reform Club should be given an opportunity of contributing to the talks given in the radio programmes. This perseverance led to a useful conclusion in May 1947, when I received an invitation to meet Sam Pollock, a BBC producer who was currently arranging a series of talks under the general title 'We Beg to Differ'. A script was written setting out our views on the future development of a payments system to encourage and develop international trade. It was based on *A Twentieth Century Economic System*.

The script was finally approved and the talk was given on the Third Programme on 9 September, 1947. Subsequently published in *The Listener*, the talk gained a worldwide circulation and resulted in a mass of correspondence from all over the world as well as from the UK, and there were very few criticisms of the view put forward. The success of this venture led to Sam Pollock suggesting that I should give a series of talks on overseas trade, which I immediately began to prepare, believing that this was a tremendous opportunity. Unfortunately, at the critical moment Pollock was transferred to another programme and the proposal fell through.

As the proposals made still have some validity the text of the broadcast is included in this book as Appendix II. I came upon an interesting sidelight some time after the broadcast when I met another BBC producer who was concerned with overseas talks, particularly to Commonwealth countries. He was complaining about the lack of freedom in selecting talks to put on overseas programmes which he had encountered. He gave as an example one talk in which he had been particularly interested as it gave a fresh viewpoint on a highly topical subject. This had been turned down at the conference where the subject had been discussed on the grounds that the speaker who had broadcast the talk was a 'crank'. To my amusement I then discovered that the talk proved to be my own contribution to 'We Beg to Differ'.

Another contributor to this series was L. St Clair Grondona, who spoke on the need for the setting up of a price-stabilising corporation. I did not know 'Gron', as his friends called him at that time, but subsequently we became great friends. I greatly admired his persistence in pursuing his scheme over many years, during which time he gained the support of many leading economists, including Lord Kaldor, Sir Roy Harrod, Lord Robert Hall and Donald Tyerman.

Subsequently I was able to broadcast on a number of occasions but always found a marked resistance to new ideas. For example, I wrote a script at the suggestion of one BBC producer on the subject of 'Where Money Comes From'. It so happened that *The Times* had published a letter from me suggesting that this whole subject was shrouded in mystery and few people could give a satisfactory explanation. So the producer suggested that I took the opportunity of writing a script to elucidate the

matter, and I took him at his word. Writing carefully in lay-
man's language, I described the orthodox textbook explanation
of how money was created and duly submitted it to the BBC.
Weeks went by, and finally I was told that the question was too
complicated to put out in a radio talk. I was so annoyed that I
published the text of the script as a pamphlet, with an intro-
ductory note setting out exactly what had happened. I sold a
large number of copies but was not very popular with the BBC
for some considerable time afterwards.

As my health improved, it became necessary to find some
way of earning a living, as all my work for economic reform was
still on an entirely voluntary basis, I even paid most of the
expenses I incurred in day-to-day activities from my own
pocket.

I was very much helped at this time by Lord Sempill. He was
a good friend and I recall his many kindnesses, not only to me
but to those with whom he came into contact. One day when I
was lunching with him at the Athenaeum Club at Christmas, he
insisted on going into the kitchen to wish all the staff a happy
Christmas. He enquired about their families and obviously took
a personal interest in their problems. This was typical. An
insight into the way he was regarded was on an occasion when I
went to see him at the House of Lords. The policeman on duty
told me there was no room in the car park, but when I told him
that I had an appointment with Lord Sempill, he said, 'That's
different', and assisted me to leave my car in an empty
space.

Realising that I faced a difficult financial problem when I had
lost not only my income but also had been refused a pension by
Cable and Wireless, he gave me a number of introductions.
One was to Nicholas Sandor, an inventor of Hungarian extrac-
tion. Sandor was the inventor of the Synchrophone system for
training and education, which combined sound with vision and
could be used with or without an instructor. This was particularly valuable to the services, and the RAF divided its
instruction between films and the Synchrophone. It was also
used by the Navy.

As a result of this introduction I became Sandor's part-time
personal assistant, and helped him not only in the development

of the Synchrophone but also with other inventions. One production of which I was particularly proud was for the National
Birthday Trust on 'The Birth of a Baby'. As I made a recording
for this, it was quite an experience to sit in a maternity ward
watching the mothers listening to my voice telling them what to
do! I also enjoyed producing a Safety picture which we made
for the Persian staff of the Anglo-Iranian Oil Company.

Some of Sandor's proposed inventions were really extra-
ordinary. I remember one plan was to use barrage balloons to
set up platforms for patients suffering from tuberculosis. It was
an interesting if somewhat tiring assignment, as I was still under
medical treatment. In due course I went before a number of
Army medical boards, who regularly turned me down for active
service.

The entire resources of the Synchrophone Company was
devoted to the war effort and when peace finally came, little had
been done to promote the Synchrophone in industrial circles.
Although a number of industries were interested, the amount
allocated by industry for spending on training seemed always to
be minimal. When it came to advertising, the sky seemed the
limit. Hence, the development tended to go in the latter direction, which I felt was a waste of a useful technique badly needed
to retrain men and women returning from the forces. Finally,
with the death of Nicholas Sandor, I retired from the scene.

I was still faced, therefore, with finding some means of raising an income. I had developed a service for members of the
Economic Reform Club during the war of supplying Parliamentary Reports covering questions and debates on economic and
financial questions. This had proved popular, and I now
decided to put this service on a more formal and personal basis
by publishing fortnightly Parliamentary Reports on the subjects
of Housing and Building; Agriculture and Food Production;
Transport; Economics and Finance and Export Policy. In the
changing political scene of the late 1940s, when so much was in
the melting pot, many leading industrial groups, banks,
insurance companies, farmers and agricultural bodies as well
as local authorities and even one or two Government depart-
ments found the reports useful, and a worthwhile subscribers'
list was built up. The reports, which were issued each fortnight,

without a break from 1947 to 1977, meant that I had read *Hansard* daily for thirty years, and it was with great regret that rising costs and other problems made it necessary to discontinue a service which I know was valued.

It was shortly after the war that I first met Captain George Drummond, of Drummond's Bank. Although a banker himself, he was a critic of the way the financial system operated and we became very friendly. He had sold out his estates in England and, like many other wealthy people, he had moved to the Isle of Man for tax reasons. He flew over to London quite frequently and we often met for discussions on monetary and economic policy.

On one occasion I lunched with him at the Savoy, and when the waiter came to take the order he dived into a bag he was carrying and produced a homemade whole-wheat loaf, which he handed to the waiter to be sliced up. He then produced a dish with butter, which he announced was home-produced. I thought this was a bit odd for the Savoy, but the waiter carried on without raising an eyebrow.

During lunch, George Drummond announced his intention to stand for election to the island parliament, the House of Keys. He wanted me to act as his adviser on economic and monetary matters and I agreed to do this. After lunch we walked up to Trafalgar Square to a branch of Drummond's Bank, where the arrival of 'Mister George' created a bit of a stir. He went to one of the tellers and whispered in his ear, whereupon a stack of those lovely crisp white £10 notes appeared and the teller proceeded to peel off five of them and handed them to me. This, I was told, was a donation to the Economic Reform Club in recognition of my assistance in the election.

The sequel was that I was telephoned from the Isle of Man regularly each morning at breakfast-time to answer all kinds of questions, and I began to feel that it was I who should have had the fifty pounds! However, George was duly elected and I was able to attend one or two sessions of the Manx Parliament in the following period. It was at the time that the proposal to issue their own currency notes was under consideration, which naturally interested me very much.

I made several visits to the island as George Drummond's guest. He was a great racing man and at one time owned a horse called 'No Fiddling'. On my last visit he told me that he had put £10 on the horse for me and it had won at useful odds. Subsequently he presented me with my winnings, but this was the last occasion that I saw him, as he died shortly after.

7

RURAL RECONSTRUCTION

The Economic Reform Club had many members who were interested in farming and agriculture. They believed that an essential element in the reforms required to put Britain on the right economic path was to arrest the serious decay in our rural and agricultural life brought about by Government policies in the inter-war years. An agricultural Committee was formed, and a close association established with a small but vigorous association called the Rural Reconstruction Association (RRA), whose objects were to secure the restoration of agriculture to its rightful place in our national life.

This Association was founded by Montague Fordham in 1926. Fordham was called 'The Sage of Seer Green', for he lived at Seer Green, in Buckinghamshire, for the last years of his life. Born in 1864, he had observed the way in which agriculture and food production had been allowed to decay in Britain, and he spent many years of devoted and selfless service in an effort to remedy this situation. His warnings over a period of thirty years that the nation's economy was not healthily balanced and that dangers lay ahead were not heeded until the outbreak of the Second World War.

Many of the reforms which were subsequently introduced in the sphere of agriculture in the 1930s and 1940s stemmed from the constructive proposals which Montague Fordham had put forward in his writings over the years from 1907, when his first book *Mother Earth* was published.

From 1926 until his death in 1948 he worked, virtually single-handedly to make the RRA into an organisation to carry out his aims, and his inspiration brought many leading people to support his efforts. Without adequate funds, however, he was unable to answer one very important question—how far could Britain feed herself.

It was left to some of us to attempt to deal with this question after his death. By great good fortune we came into touch with Dr J. J. Grace, who lived in the USA but was on a visit to Britain, as he had inherited a considerable sum in sterling. As he was sufficiently wealthy not to want these additional resources, he had decided to use this money to assist organisations in Britain concerned with rural economics that he thought needed additional financial help. It was Derek Stuckey, a member of the Economic Reform Club who was also an Executive of the RRA, who first made contact with Dr Grace at the Farmer's Club in London. Further meetings were arranged and as a result he made available a considerable sum to enable the RRA to carry out a major work of research into the extent which Britain could be self-supporting in food.

The Research Committee of the RRA which worked on this report had been set up in 1947, and the first report by this Committee was published in 1950. This paved the way for the more substantial study published in 1955 by Hollis and Carter. The Chairman of the Research Committee was Alan Hawkins, but the major part of the work of research was carried out by Derek Stuckey, ably assisted by Jorian Jenks, who prepared the report on which the final study was based. I was a member of the small drafting sub-committee which revised and approved the final text and I know the immense amount of voluntary work which went into producing this.

The Report set out to answer two important questions:
(1) What steps would have to be taken to secure a substantial increase in home agricultural production of food?
(2) What main changes in consumption would be indicated if it were necessary to rely mainly on food produced at home?

The conclusions reached were that, given the right kind of economic climate, we could increase the extent to which we could go in producing our own food from the generally accepted figure of 50 per cent to at least 75 or even 85 per cent, a figure which has subsequently proved correct.

Having produced the report, we then needed to find a title for the book as well as a publisher. I recall that it was when I was busily engaged in harvesting the potato crop in my garden on the South Coast that I hit on what seemed to me to be the ideal title for a book dealing with food production: *Feeding the Fifty Million*. My colleagues agreed, and I was subsequently able to get Hollis and Carter to publish the book, which was finally produced in March 1955. *The Times Survey of British Agriculture for March 1955* described it as 'A well-informed account of the scope there is for the increased home production of food'. *The British Farmer* said that it contained 'a most thorough survey of the problems involved, as well as a stimulating and highly valuable set of proposals'. There were many other reviews in similar vein.

The funds provided by Dr Grace also enabled the Economic Reform Club and the RRA to extend the scope and circulation of a journal, jointly sponsored by the two organisations, entitled *Rural Economy*. Edited by Jorian Jenks for some years, I joined him as Joint Editor in 1954. Looking back at some of the issues published nearly thirty years ago it is astonishing to find so many problems which are still with us today.

The last issue of *Rural Economy* appeared in October–November 1956 and the Editorial Notes which appeared in this issue are perhaps relevant to this story.

For 30 and 20 years respectively, the Rural Reconstruction Association and the Economic Reform Club have played a significant part in the life of the nation. Though relatively small bodies, they have striven constantly and often effectively to bring the clear light of well-informed commonsense to bear upon those superficial assessments and stock phrases which are so apt to pass for axioms in a mass-democracy. Events are demonstrating the continuing need for such efforts. This, therefore, seems an appropriate occasion on which to summarise the objectives of the two bodies.

The RRA will always be associated with the memory of Montague Fordham, one of the most clear-headed and original thinkers of our times. Commencing his campaign at a period when British agriculture, ham-strung by the 1914–18 post-war deflation and the sudden repeal of the 1920 Agriculture Act, was virtually being written-off, he lobbied and wrote persistently against so defeatist a view. He not only argued most lucidly that a stable and productive rural economy was essential to the well-being of the whole community; he showed in simple terms how this object could be achieved.

Foremost among his proposals he placed the principle of standard prices for staple farm products, as opposed to the fluctuations of the open market. But he also maintained that agriculturists of all classes and parties should be united in a comprehensive body capable of presenting and helping to solve agriculture's own problems. For he had little faith in party politics, academic economics or industrial mentality so far as agrarian matters were concerned. His ripe experience in more than one country led him to favour the small working farmer, carrying on the peasant tradition, rather than the big capitalist entrepreneur, as the most important element in rural development; but he was never dogmatic on such points.

Incidentally, he must have been one of the first in modern times to challenge the assumption implicit in almost all contemporary economic thought and policy, namely, that all trade is beneficial. His attitude was that trade, like most other economic activities, was functional and must be judged on its merits, not seen as an end in itself.

Those whom Fordham gathered round him to form the RRA included some of the most thoughtful people in public life, and their influence on national policy has been far from negligible. Beginning with the Wheat Act of 1932, which first incorporated the principle of a standard price, the broad trend of agricultural policy ever since has been in the direction that Fordham advocated. For example, the 'guaranteed' price figured prominently in the 1947 Agriculture Act; and though widely misinterpreted often misapplied and recently much modified, it has come to be regarded by the great majority of farmers and farm workers as the sheet-anchor of their economic security.

In keeping with its tradition of 'getting at the facts', the RRA revived, after the war, its research committee, instructing it to assemble information as to the extent to which Britain could actually feed herself if the need arose, and the steps best calculated to secure this end. Owing to the size and complexity of such an investigation, the committee's final report, published as *Feeding the Fifty Million*, could not be issued till last year. By that date, public interest in the subject had waned considerably, owing to a progressive easing in the food situation. But the report was widely noticed and found its way into official circles. It may yet prove of considerable value of reference and guidance; for with the world in its present state, there can be no lasting security in any real sense for a country that must import half the food it eats.

The Economic Reform Club has always taken a similar stand for enlightened commonsense, especially in monetary policy. Difficult and unattractive as such a subject must seem to most people, the Club nevertheless aroused widespread interest and support in the late 1930s by pin-pointing the prime cause of economic depression and unemployment—insufficiency of monetary purchasing power in consumers' pockets. It exposed the fallacies of a policy of 'sound finance' which sought to bolster up the exchange value of the £ by reducing the number of £s in domestic circulation, and showed that economic problems could not be attributed to over-production so long as millions of people were existing at subsistence level, but arose in fact from under-consumption.

After the war, with inflation rather than deflation the main disability, the ERC campaigned vigorously against the subordination of our economy to the dollar system through the Bretton Woods Agreement and the Washington Loan. This again was commonsense. Preoccupation with the 'dollar gap' has been a grave handicap to the economic development of the Commonwealth and has entangled Britain in the restrictions of GATT without ever achieving its avowed object of sterling convertibility.

The ERC includes among its supporters MPs and prominent persons of all parties and of none. Essentially, it provides a forum for the objective discussion of economic matters. But frequently issues arise on which agreement among its members and friends is so marked that concerted action can be taken through Parliament and the press.

Recently, for example, the Club has been critical of the 'credit-squeeze' as an unjust and largely ineffective weapon against inflation. The real remedy for inflation, it maintains, lies primarily in the Government's own hands, through the better ordering of its financing and more direct control over the volume of money in circulation. This second point has always featured largely in its educational work; for without a well-adjusted relationship between purchasing power and the current volume of production, there will always be alternations of boom and slump, inflation and deflation, labour-scarcity and unemployment.

Thus the outlook of the Rural Reconstruction Association and of the Economic Reform Club have reflected, and still reflect, many points of similarity. For it is just as essential, in the national interest, to restore money to its rightful place as the servant (not the dictator) of the social economy as it is to restore agriculture to its rightful place in our national life.

By keeping such principles, together with the technical considerations they involve, constantly before an intelligent section of the public, RURAL ECONOMY, we believe, has been doing work of some national importance.

8

AN ECONOMIC MILESTONE

For a short while I became prospective Parliamentary candidate in Brighton and Hove, but finally decided to contest the Ealing North constituency in the 1950 election. Once again, the local Liberal organisation was very weak and, although the campaign had its moments, I did not poll enough votes to save my deposit. By this time I was somewhat disillusioned with party politics, and came to the conclusion that I could probably do more good in a non-party capacity by continuing to press for the economic reforms which seemed to be even more necessary in the post-war world. Unfortunately, however, the defeat which the Economic Reform Club had sustained over the Washington Loan and Bretton Woods Agreement disheartened many of our supporters. Confronted by the many problems which arose in the period after the war, they seemed to be less inclined to be concerned with economic questions in the national and international context.

Antony Vickers, cousin of Vincent Vickers, had become President of the Club in 1946 and I worked very closely with him in an effort to overcome this fading support and membership. We jointly sponsored a number of private dinner parties when we met some leading trade union officials. We were greatly helped in this by Victor Feather, then deputy to George Woodcock, the General Secretary of the TUC. In private conversation with these trade union leaders we found a great deal of common ground, but it became obvious that while they were ready to recognise the problems, they were unable to give any official blessing to the economic reforms we advocated.

We were confronted with the problem of trying to find some other central premises, as the house we had occupied in Muswell Hill since 1942 was now required by the owners for development. By arrangement with the Rev. Patrick McLaughlin, the Warden, we were able to use St Anne's House in Soho as a central address while the work was carried out at a small office in Muswell Hill.

In an effort to re-establish some Club facilities, we opened a restaurant on the first floor of St Anne's House in Dean Street, Soho, by arrangement with the Rev. Patrick McLaughlin. This was open to members of the Economic Reform Club and also to local people who joined the St Anne's Club, which we formed. Rationing was still in force and this very much limited our menus. Nevertheless, for a time this venture was a great success. An example of the problems which arise when venturing into the catering business was illustrated when in the middle of lunch I was called to the kitchen to deal with the cook, who was throwing marmalade puddings out of the window at passing pedestrians in Dean Street.

It was unfortunate for us, however, that the manageress and cook who had done so much to help us build up a regular clientele both left at the same time, just as I was leaving for a series of lecture engagements. The replacements, hastily engaged to fill the gap, were a disaster. So we lost our clientele and had no alternative but to close down this facility. Membership of the Club had steadily declined from nearly 2000 at the end of the war to about 350 in 1949.

The Economic Research Council had, among its other activities, sponsored a monthly journal under the title *Economic Digest*. This was first produced in 1946, edited by Sir Geoffrey Bracken. It had undergone a number of management changes and finally, in 1954, at the suggestion of Lady Rhys Williams, it was taken over by Dr Wallersteiner, who was prepared to put up the funds necessary for survival.

John (now Sir John) Biggs-Davison, who shortly afterwards became MP for Chigwell, was appointed Editor and asked me to join him as Joint Editor. We met regularly at the House of Commons and I found it an absorbing task. Circulation continued to grow and then, out of the blue, we were confronted with the fact that Dr Wallersteiner could no longer provide the funds to subsidise the publication. Some debts had been incurred and it took us some time to clear these. Finally we solved the problem by selling Economic Digest Ltd and the title

Economic Digest, which provided the funds to pay off all outstanding debts. We continued to publish the journal under the title *Commonwealth Digest & World Economic Review* until the journal was taken over by Laurence French Publications.

This activity had brought me, once again, into closer touch with the Economic Research Council and its activities. In 1953 they had published an important paper entitled 'The Child on the Road', which had given them a great deal of useful publicity. Some dissatisfaction had subsequently been expressed at the publication of pámphlets dealing with teenage drunkenness and it was felt that these were hardly the kind of publications which the Economic Research Council should be solely identified with. With the ending of the two Covenants which had sustained the Council for the past seven years it was no longer possible to pay staff, and Harold Goodwin, who had been the mainstay of the organisation, decided that he wanted to enter Holy Orders.

Realising that the Economic Reform Club membership was still dwindling (it was down to 90 in 1954) I realised that the chances of achieving its long-term object of getting an enquiry into the workings of the economic and monetary system were becoming remote. When it was suggested that I should take over as Honorary Secretary of the Economic Research Council in addition to the Club I accepted, and I have now completed over thirty years in this capacity.

Four years later, in 1959, I proposed that the Economic Reform Club and Institute should establish closer links with the Council. While maintaining a separate existence, the two bodies should work together towards their common objective. This has proved a successful arrangement, though the Council is now established as a strong organisation and the Club has declined to only a few members.

A short while after this arrangement was agreed, we were advised by the trustees of the Will of the late Dr Peart of Northumberland that he had left the Economic Reform Club as a residual legatee to his estate together with the National Trust. The trustees advised that the amount likely to be available was in the region of £37,000, which would certainly have enabled us to put the Club on the map once again. However, this matter is still unresolved.

As previously indicated, the main objective of the Economic Reform Club was to get an enquiry into the workings of the economic and monetary system. With the support of the two organisations we decided to initiate a further effort to obtain such an investigation. Our first shot in this campaign was to draft a letter to *The Times*, which I took along to Printing House Square. I discussed it with Donald Tyerman, then Deputy Editor, and he told me that the letter was important and that we should proceed to get an influential list of signatories, in which case he would ensure that the letter was published. The following is the text of the letter as finally agreed:

The Editor,
The Times

Sir,
Now that the Chancellor has produced his autumn budget, and the debates in Parliament have taken place on the measures proposed, we feel that the time has come to reconsider our economic and monetary policy and its effect on the lives and welfare of the people living in these islands. It is clear from the speeches made that few of the political leaders fully understand the measures which should be taken to deal with persistent inflation and balance of payments difficulties.

We agree that our prime need is increased production. Yet can it be said that the measures now proposed provide for the necessary incentive for both managers and men and indeed all sections of the community to give of their best and thus maintain the soundness of sterling and the vigour of the British economy? On the contrary, there is much evidence of uncertainty and confusion, the presentation of further wage demands, and the danger of strikes if they are not granted. There is no need to insist on the disastrous consequences to our economy of such a situation.

There is a lack of confidence that the measures proposed will produce stability in our economic life. It is essential that the cost of living should be stabilised, that the steady deterioration in the purchasing power of the pound sterling should be arrested and producers of all kinds encouraged to increase output with reasonable assurance that it will find a market. These objects command general assent; the means of achieving them are much less apparent. Even the Governor of the Bank of England has voiced doubts when he said—

'We have still to find the ideal measures to reinforce monetary policy to make it work better and more quickly.'

We therefore urge that an enquiry be set up without delay to examine the workings of our financial system in its internal, Commonwealth and international aspects. If Her Majesty's Government in the United Kingdom were to institute such an inquiry they would be pursuing a similar course to that now being followed by Her Majesty's Government in New Zealand and Canada, countries which are experiencing similar economic difficulties.

The signatories to the letter were: Archer Baldwin, MP (Con.); C. R. Bence, MP (Lab.); John Biggs-Davison, MP (Con.); Sir Robert Boothby, MP (Con.); L. S. Dawson, Managing Director of the Oil Well Engineering Co.; Bob Edwards, MP (Lab.); Lysaght Finigan, Editor of *Shipping*; Jo Grimond, MP (Lib.); John Penton, Chairman of the Economic Research Council; Lady Rhys Williams; Lord Sempill; R. R. Stokes, MP (Lab.); Antony Vickers, of Fluidrive Engineering, and myself.

The Times duly published the letter in November, 1955. This started off a considerable campaign. Deputations to the Federation of British Industries and other bodies were arranged in an effort to whip up industrial support.

It was interesting to note that Sir Norman Kipping of the FBI, who received the deputation with Mr Arthur Shenfield (then Economic Adviser to the Federation), took the view that such an enquiry as we envisaged was completely unnecessary. I had been invited to lead the deputation by L. S. Dawson, and I did my best to convince Sir Norman that there were many things wrong with the economy, mainly stemming from a faulty monetary mechanism, but he was adamant that all was well and that we were wasting our time in urging that an enquiry should be set up. This was typical of many of those in industry who seemed quite incapable of looking beyond the immediate future.

Fortunately, there were others who took a more realistic view than the FBI. We were encouraged to send a follow-up letter to

The Times which was published on 22 February 1957. In it we suggested that events since the publication of our original letter had underlined the need for an enquiry into the workings of the monetary system and that this should be undertaken as a matter of urgency. It was signed by 12 MPs, peers and industrialists.

Following this we formed a group of MPs of all parties under the title of Parliamentary and Industrial Committee of the Economic Research Council. Sir Robert (later Lord) Boothby was the Chairman, Douglas (later Lord) Houghton Vice-Chairman and John Biggs-Davison and myself as joint Honorary Secretaries. This group decided to ask the Chancellor of the Exchequer, then Harold Macmillan, to receive a deputation and the following letter was sent.

> At a meeting of the all-Party Parliamentary and Industrial Committee held in the House of Commons this week it was agreed to write you a letter urging that immediate steps be taken to set up an impartial enquiry, on the lines of the Macmillan Committee, to examine the working of the financial system in its internal, Commonwealth and international aspects.
>
> There is widespread belief that the statistical information at present available to the Government is inadequate, and that the existing financial machinery is no longer an effective instrument for carrying out the national economic policy.
>
> We should be grateful if you would be good enough to receive a small deputation from our Committee.

Sir Robert Boothby, Douglas Houghton, Jo Grimond, Nicholas Davenport, Antony Vickers and myself were duly appointed to serve as members of the deputation and we presented ourselves to the Chancellor in his private room at the House of Commons on Tuesday, 20 March 1956.

I had rather expected to find a bevy of Treasury experts to meet us but in fact Mr Macmillan, with one assistant to take notes, met us and he invited us all in turn to state our case. He devoted a full hour to the deputation and listened with care to the views we put forward in support of our request for an impartial enquiry.

The main points were:

(1) That our statistical system is inadequate to enable the

Government to judge with sufficient precision or accuracy
future economic trends;

(2) That our monetary and banking system does not meet the
requirements of modern economic theory and practice;
and

(3) That the existing machinery for carrying out the economic
policy of the Government leaves much to be desired.

The first point was generously conceded by Mr Macmillan
and in his Budget speech on 17 April 1956, he made reference
to the views of the deputation, saying:

> I am told that some of our statistics are too late to be as useful as
> they ought to be. We are always, as it were, looking up a train in
> last year's *Bradshaw*.

He went on to agree that in the area of statistical information
'some improvement can and should be made'. On the question
of an investigation into monetary policy he said:

> I am considering this all very carefully, and, as soon as more
> immediate preoccupations are out of the way, I hope to make
> progress.

The final outcome was the announcement by Peter
Thorneycroft, by then Chancellor of the Exchequer, of the decision to set up the Radcliffe Committee on Credit and Currency,
which finally reported in 1959. This was undoubtedly an
economic milestone and a major victory in our long-standing
campaign started in 1936 to obtain an impartial investigation
into the workings of the monetary system. Members of our
Parliamentary and Industrial Committee were exultant, and we
had a celebration lunch presided over by Bob Boothby, which
was a very hilarious occasion.

When the setting up of the Radcliffe Committee was announced, Bob Boothby went on the radio and made the rather
rash claim that this would save the country. He did, however,
have the courtesy to telephone me before he made the broadcast to thank me for the part I had played. Many of my friends,

in particular John Langdon-Davis, took a rather sour view of the fact that he did not give any of those associated with him any credit for the outcome. However, the important thing was that at last we had got the enquiry set up.

Unfortunately, however, the Radcliffe Report, when finally published, was a grave disappointment. It was obvious that no attention had been paid to the evidence which Antony Vickers and I had submitted. A similar submission made by Niall McDermot (subsequently Financial Secretary to the Treasury) and Arthur Fountain was also ignored.

The most valuable part of the exercise was the publication of three volumes of evidence which had been submitted to the Commission. The evidence submitted by the Bank of England and the Treasury provided an important clarification of the way the monetary system operated. As a result it could no longer be claimed that banks did not create credit as had been argued by the President of the Institute of Bankers in Scotland back in the war years. Our view which had been condemned as being 'misdirected, misconceived and mischievious' were shown to be correct and were abundantly confirmed by the Bank of England in its evidence. In the section dealing with the Control of Bank Credit in UK it said:

> Because an entry in the books of a bank has come to be generally accepted in place of cash it is possible for the banks to create the equivalent of cash [i.e. credit]. Thus a bank may pay for a security purchased from a customer merely by making an entry in its books to the credit of that customer's account; or it may make an advance by means of a similar entry. In either case, an increase in its deposits will occur.

Later it stated:

> if the Exchequer borrows by issuing Treasury Bills which are taken up by the banks and spends the proceeds (so that the cash borrowed finds its way back to the banks) the liquid assets and deposits of the banks will be increased and they will be put in a position to increase the supply of bank credit. Indeed, because only a proportion of the banks' deposits requires to be covered by cash and other liquid assets, a given loss or gain of liquid assets by the banks has an effect several times as great on the potential volume of bank credit.

So, after thirty years of campaigning we did get the record set straight on this important question about money creation. The Radcliffe Report itself was, however, a bitter disappointment. The members of the Committee had obviously been bogged down by the complexity of the problems they confronted. Commenting on their failure to provide any satisfactory conclusions W. T. Newlyn of the Department of Economics at Leeds University wrote:

> The Radcliffe Committee did not merely reject the quantity theory of money: it rejected money itself in a significant sense. The really distinctive feature of the Radcliffe Report is not that it emphasised that exclusive concentration on the quantity of money was wrong, but that in doing so it denied that money had any special significance at all . . . we view it as only part of the wider structure of liquidity (para. 389). It is this view, reflected right throughout the Report, that justifies the complaint that Radcliffe threw out the baby with the bath-water or, to adapt the metaphor, drowned the baby with an excess of liquidity. (*Money in Britain*, 1959–69, edited by R. Croome and Harry G. Johnson, OUP, 1970).

In an article commenting on the Radcliffe Report I wrote:

> The Report says that 'spending is not limited by the amount of money in existence, but it is related to the amount of money people think they can get hold of . . .' Surely this points to the moral that somewhere in the monetary mechanism a regulator is needed to replace gold to prevent more money coming into existence than is required to maintain a healthy and balanced economy? Otherwise what is to prevent expansion developing into inflation? As people begin to feel wealthier they demand more and more money. In addition, they spend what they have at a faster rate. Unless some realistic regulator is at work to determine the extent to which the supply of money can safely be increased, inflation is the inevitable outcome. Once inflation gets out of hand remedial measures have to be so strong that they tend to put the economy into reverse and recession will threaten.

This comment was written twenty-one years ago. Bearing in mind what is happening in the 1980s these words were surely prophetic.

In 1938, just before war broke out, a friend of mine, Desmond Allhusen, had written a book entitled *The Master Problem*, in which he had explained a great deal about money and its development over the years. I had found this a very interesting source of information, and in 1958 Desmond and I decided to work together on a book which not only gave the historical background but also suggested specific reforms to the monetary system.

Desmond lived in Somerset and I was still working in London, but somehow we managed to work together to produce a book to which we gave the title *Money the Decisive Factor*.

We approached Dr Mc. I. Johnson, who was a publisher and the MP for Carlisle, and he agreed to accept the book, which was published in May 1959. We arranged a launching party at the House of Commons, sponsored by Dr Johnson, and although we could not claim that it was extensively reviewed, it did get some space in the national press.

The first edition sold out by September 1960 and we then brought a second edition in October 1960. As we said in the preface to the second edition,

> In preparing our Second Edition we have had the benefit of the up-to-date and exhaustive review of the monetary system provided by the Radcliffe Report, and we have therefore made extensive additions to our chapter IV, 'What Money Is'. The report leaves no room for dispute about the manner in which the system works, or for doubt about the damage which it has inflicted on our more progressive industries. But where the Report is disappointing is that, having described so clearly the nature of the problem, the authors confess that they are unable to offer a complete solution—one that would 'constitute real protection of the currency'.

The famous historian, Sir Arthur Bryant, contributed the foreword to the book. He wrote:

> Money is the elastic instrument by which free men translate their needs into the production of the goods they require. The proper flow and distribution of money is, therefore, vital if a free society is to operate properly. If in a free society anything goes wrong with its

financial system, everything else will go wrong and freedom itself will be brought into disrepute and endangered.

The book continued to sell reasonably well and we were able to publish two paperback editions. It was also translated into Japanese and duly published in that country.

It is perhaps appropriate to include a slightly edited version of the chapter from *Money the Decisive Factor* under the title 'What Money Is', for although there have been alterations and amendments to the money system since the book was published in 1959 the basic criticisms remain. In particular, the reasons for our disappointment with the Radcliffe Committee Report are set out in some detail. As we said in the preface to the second edition, 'where the Report is disappointing is that, having described so clearly the nature of the problem, the authors confess that they are unable to offer a complete solution—one that would 'constitute real protection' of the currency.

9

WHAT MONEY IS

A major event in monetary history occurred in August 1914 when the First World War began. The gold standard was immediately suspended and the Currency and Bank Notes Act was passed through Parliament in a single day. The sovereigns and half sovereigns were withdrawn and Postal Orders were made legal tender while the Treasury Notes were being printed. At first everything went smoothly enough, and it appeared that the Government had the situation well in hand.

The events that followed make depressing reading. Without doubt the Government's intentions were excellent, but they had hopelessly underestimated the strength of the temptation to exploit money. Even men who in every other respect were scrupulously honest appeared to be unable to resist it.

Briefly, what happened was this. The Government brought in an Act which allowed the banks to draw the new Treasury Notes up to a maximum of 20 per cent of their liabilities. The banks drew their notes, and for a time everything went according to plan. Then, to save trouble, the Treasury began to give the banks certificates for larger amounts, and after that it apparently forgot all about the limit of 20 per cent and allowed them to buy as many as they wanted and to pay for them by giving drafts on their own credit. 'In this way the principle of limitation as applied to the notes was practically abandoned. What ought to have been barriers to expansion became elastic bands that yielded at the slightest pressure. The reserves were adjusted to the liabilities and not the liabilities to the real reserves. In place of a limited amount of gold that could only be increased by being attracted from other countries, the real banking reserve was now a mass of notes which could be increased on the demand of the banks themselves.'*

* 'Inflation', Professor J. S. Nicholson. *Encyclopaedia Britannica*: 12th Edition.

The position therefore was that the banks used their credit to buy Treasury Notes, and then used the notes as the base for a further creation of credit. In addition to this, the Government insisted on following the traditional but entirely unnecessary practice of borrowing from the Bank of England whenever they were short of money, and as the war cost a great deal more than the taxes produced, they had to borrow very heavily. When in due course the Government paid out the money which they had borrowed and the recipients paid it into their own banks, the bankers immediately added it to the base on which they built their pyramids of credit. The Committee on Currency and Foreign Exchanges which was appointed after the war explained the whole process very clearly, and in view of the disastrous results which were to follow we consider it advisable to quote their Report at some length. There should be no room for misunderstanding as to what really happened.

Suppose, for example, in a given week the Government require £10 million over and above receipts from taxes and loans from the public. They apply for an advance from the Bank of England, which by a book entry places the amount required to the credit of public deposits. The amount is then paid out to Government creditors, and passes, when the cheques are cleared, to the credit of their bankers in the books of the Bank of England—in other words, is transferred from 'Public' to 'Other' deposits, the effect of the whole transaction thus being to increase by £10 million the purchasing power in the hands of the public in the form of deposits in the joint stock banks and the bankers' cash at the Bank of England by the same amount. The bankers' liabilities to depositors having thus increased by £10 million and their cash reserves by an equal amount, their proportion of cash to liabilities (which was normally before the war something under 20 per cent) is improved, with the result that they are in a position to make advances to their customers to an amount equal to four or five times the sum added to their cash reserves, or, in the absence of demand for such accommodation, to increase their investments by the difference between the cash received and the proportion they require to hold against the increase of their deposit liabilities. Since the outbreak of war it is the second procedure which has in the main been followed, the surplus cash having been used to subscribe for Treasury Bills and other Government securities. The money so subscribed has again been spent by the Government and returned in the manner described to the bankers' cash balances, the process being repeated again and again, until each £10 million originally advanced by the Bank of England has created new deposits representing new purchasing power to several times that amount.

Throughout the war the banks made full use of their opportunities to create credit: they then used it to buy War Loan and other Government securities or to make private loans. When the war ended they held about £360 million more than they had held when it began, while their loans of various kinds had risen from £540 million to £1263 million. It thus happened that one result of the war which nobody had expected was that the country found itself compelled to pay a vast annual tribute of interest to the banks.

Although the wartime governments certainly failed badly in the supervision of finance, they at least had the excuse that they had other things to think about. It is not however so easy to excuse the almost unbelievable mistakes which were made after the war. The position was that the internal war debt totalled about £6000 million, and a great deal of it was owed, either directly or indirectly, to the banks. If the debt had been more or less evenly spread over the whole country it would have been an entirely different matter, as debtors and creditors would then have been the same people; but of course it was not. As long as there was this great load of debt to carry it should have been clear that the only hope of keeping the country solvent and reasonably prosperous was to maintain an adequate supply of money, and moreover to ensure that it was allowed to circulate freely. Above all it should have been clear that it would be fatal to reduce the volume of money in circulation until the debt had been reduced in proportion. But this was exactly what the government did: they reduced the supply of money until the pound had doubled in value, and left the debt untouched. The experts — that is, the Bank of England, who had their own reasons for wanting the gold standard — were insistent that we should get back to it as quickly as possible, and the Government meekly did what they told them to. By 1925 the price level had fallen 50 per cent and it was considered safe to return to gold.

At that time Mr Churchill was Chancellor of the Exchequer and he has given his own account of what happened: 'When I was moved by many arguments and forces in 1925 to return to the gold standard, I was assured by the highest experts that we were anchoring ourselves to reality and stability, and I accepted their advice. But what has happened? We have no reality, no stability. The price of gold has risen since then by more than seventy per cent. Look at the enormously increased volume of commodities which have to be created in order to pay off the same mortgage, debt or loan. This monetary convulsion has now reached a pitch where I am persuaded that the producers of new wealth will not tolerate indefinitely so hideous an oppression'.

In the post-war world there were plenty of factors unfavourable to British exports, and it might have been supposed that the Government would do everything in their power to ensure that manufacturers could at least rely on a good home market. But nothing, it seemed, was allowed to delay the return to the gold standard. The natural result of their policy was the Great Depression. There was never the slightest mystery about its causes. The country was paying large sums of interest to the banks, either directly as interest or indirectly as taxes which went to pay the interest on Government loans, and this meant that people had less money to spend. The home market therefore began to suffer: manufacturers could not sell their products; factories went on short time, and the unemployment figures began to rise. Clearly the only way to put things right was for the banks to put the money back into circulation with the least possible delay so that the public could spend it. Unfortunately they did nothing of the kind. They hesitated to increase their dividends at a time when so many people were suffering hardship. Bankers talked freely about this problem in private, though not of course in public. They appeared to be overwhelmed by the vast sums of money which were pouring in. Eventually they decided on a course of action which they hoped would put everything right without attracting too much attention. They began to buy up building sites in every town in the country, selecting the best they could find, usually on corners. They built innumerable new branches, and in addition to this they built palatial head offices in the City. But building new banks was hardly the best or quickest way to get the money back into the pockets of the people who had parted with it. It was better than nothing, but it was not enough.

Meanwhile the unemployment figures continued to rise until in 1930 they nearly reached three million. The industrial areas presented a depressing spectacle. Many firms with famous names and long histories found themselves unable to carry on, and the shopkeepers suffered nearly as much as the workmen who had lost their jobs. In the end whole districts were living on the dole; the Depressed Areas had appeared. The frustration and suffering were beyond all calculation.

A great deal has been written about the causes of the Great Depression, but remarkably little has been said about the one-way traffic of money to the banks. It was apparently considered tactless to draw attention to it. But when every possible allowance has been made for every other factor, it is impossible to escape the conclusion that this traffic was the principle one. The reduced demand for our exports explains a great deal, but not everything. It does not, for instance, explain why in the home market firms and individuals with goods or services to offer suddenly found themselves unable to exchange them with each other in the traditional manner; the problems of international trade had nothing whatever to do with it. But there was no need to look far for the reason. In the present age the exchange of goods and services can only be carried out by the use of money, if there is not enough of it to go round it follows that there will be fewer exchanges. Trade cannot be carried on without an adequate supply of money. Everything needed for production: machines, skilled workmen, land, farmers, were there, ready and waiting to play their parts, but the essential link between them, money, was missing. The country had moved too far from the age of barter to find its way back, and although a number of barter schemes were in fact launched, nobody imagined that they were going to make up for the missing money. The Great Depression was no 'Act of God or the King's Enemies'; it was the inevitable result of twenty years of monetary folly.

Strangely enough, it was the King's Enemies who finally brought the Great Depression to an end. We have seen how the Victorians were lucky to obtain enough money from outside the banking system to enable them to pay the banks' interest charges and therefore remain solvent. What really saved them was of course the fact that the miners were not money-lenders; if interest-free paper money had appeared instead it would have done just as well. In the late nineteen thirties, when re-armament began in earnest, money of this kind did in fact appear. Government spending introduced vast sums of debt-free money into the economy, and although the banks used part of it as the base for further creation of credit, the flow of money was so great that there was never the slightest danger of a break-down. In fact the only danger was that, instead of there being too little money, there would be too much. This state of affairs continued throughout the war, and when the war was over the Welfare State appeared and the flood of money continued unabated.

Eventually, as we know, the volume of money rose to a fantastic level, but as long as the tap was kept running, everybody who was not trying to live on a fixed income was perfectly happy; pensioners and others whose incomes did not keep pace with prices were not so happy. But the feverish prosperity suited most people, and many were simple enough to believe that the printing press was the answer to all our problems. It was not however long before the less pleasant results of inflation began to appear. The abundance of money not only drove up prices, but it created an exaggerated demand for labour, with the result that the vital exporting industries, who had to keep their prices reasonably near the world level, were unable to get all they needed. The trade balance turned heavily against us, and the pound was devalued. The fall in the value of the pound made a mockery of savings and the gilt-edged market began to collapse. Gradually the country realized what inflation meant, and on all sides it was agreed that it must be stopped without delay.

The trouble was that there appeared to be no way of stopping inflation without landing the country in another depression. However dangerous it might be to allow the rise in prices to continue, it appeared to be even more dangerous to try to stop it. For a long time nobody even dared to use the word deflation; the Great Depression had not been forgotten. It was finally decided that the best course was to keep the supply of money at or about the existing level, and it was hoped that if this were done prices would remain steady. But unfortunately this did not work out as the Government hoped it would. Although the supply of money was restricted, prices went on rising as fast, or nearly as fast, as before and it became clear that inflation could, as it were, continue under its own steam. The reason for this is very simple: the more money there is about the faster people are likely to spend it, and when a pound note is used to make two purchases in a day instead of one, the effect on prices is exactly the same as if two pounds were being used to make one purchase each. What made the problem even more intractable than it need have been was the general observance of the taboo on the whole subject of credit-money and interest charges.

Finally the Government appointed a committee of eminent men, with Lord Cohen as chairman, in the hope that they would help to solve the problem. But so far they have given little if any reason to believe that they have found the answer. They agree, in fact, with Mr Heathcoat Amory that the best we can do is to try to maintain a precarious balance between inflation and deflation. A typical passage from their reports — it occurs in the second — is 'the dangers of inflation have only been scotched, not killed'; and again, 'past experience suggests that any substantial revival of demand may well be accompanied by renewed threats to price stability". So the prospect they offer us is not exactly a cheerful one: we must apparently continue to pick our way as best we can between the two dangers which are constantly threatening us, and which, if the Committee are right, are likely to remain with us for the rest of our lives.

It is strange that hardly a voice has been raised in protest against this depressing verdict. The objections to the Committee's reports — and there have been plenty of them — mostly came from those who accepted their general conclusions but parted company with them over the issue whether we should regard inflation or deflation as our chief danger at the moment. The Trades Union leaders were particularly angry with them; Mr Will Carron, President of the Amalgamated Engineering Union, denounced their 'retrograde suggestions' and maintained that the Trades Union Congress were right to have nothing to do with them. Up and down the country the debate between the inflationists and the deflationists continues as briskly as ever, and under the circumstances there seems little reason why it should ever stop. As long as the choice which we are offered is only one between two evils, it seems highly improbable that everybody will make the same choice.

Yet in spite of the impressive array of arguments produced on either side, it is difficult to believe that we have really been condemned to spend our days dodging about between deflation, which means having too little money, and inflation, which means having too much. Why, where money is concerned, should there be no golden mean, no sensible middle way between deficiency and excess? Surely there must be something wrong? When a problem appears to have no reasonable solution it is permissible to doubt whether it has been accurately stated. Are we perhaps trying to do a puzzle when some of the pieces do not belong? So before we go any further we had better make sure that the pieces we have got are the right ones: we had better examine the monetary system which is producing such strange and unsatisfactory results. Fortunately there is no need to thread our way through the vast maze of detail which might almost have been designed for the purpose of discouraging people from enquiring too closely into the nature of our money. All that is necessary is that we should clearly understand the general principles on which the system works.

If an examination of the monetary system is to produce results of real value, it is essential that it should cover a period long enough to allow us to see things in their true perspective. If it is confined to the present and the recent past, the most that we can expect from it is a detailed description of the trees, but we are not likely to learn very much about the wood. We will therefore choose as our starting-point the year 1844, when the Bank Charter Act became law. As we know, this Act established a system in which money was mainly gold, but authorized the Bank of England to add a strictly limited amount of paper money in the form of bank notes. But as the Bank was obliged to redeem these notes in gold they were in effect only under-studying gold. Even when the joint stock banks began to use their credit as a form of money transferred by cheque they were still bound to pay their depositors in gold if they asked for it. Thus in theory, and largely in practice, our money was gold, and so it remained until 1914. At that time no less than 66 per cent of bank notes were actually backed by gold.

The Act of 1844 is of course a dead letter: the Radcliffe Report confirms that 'The Central Principles of the 1844 legislation have been discarded. The note issue has been completely detached from the gold reserve'. But the reason why a knowledge of this Act is important is that every major change made in the course of the last century is the result, either direct or indirect, of our abandonment of its central principle, the link with gold. If we remember this we will find no difficulty in understanding a great many things which might otherwise appear incomprehensible.

In England we have always had an amiable weakness for preserving traditional forms long after they have lost their original meaning; and this is exactly what we have done with our money. As long as the gold was there, the amount of 'cover' provided for the various forms of paper money was obviously a matter of considerable importance; but today, when as far as money is concerned the gold is nothing but a beautiful memory, we still keep up the pretence that we are providing cover. Thus the Bank of England Returns show that the Note Issue is covered by Government securities, and although this may perhaps impress people who do not look too closely, all that it really means is that one kind of government paper is being covered by another kind. As they both draw their value from the same source, it follows that if one were to lose it the other would lose it too.

The position is therefore that our bank notes reach us from the printing press, their only cover consisting of something of no more value than themselves. As the banks are obliged to give their depositors notes if they ask for them, it follows that the number in circulation depends on the demand for them, and this again depends on the amount of credit-money in existence at the time. The supply of notes is therefore adjusted to the volume of credit-money, instead of, as formerly, the other way round. Credit-money is the form of money most widely used today. In theory it is covered by the banks' reserves, but as most of these are represented by investments and loans of one kind and another, which could not be turned into cash at a moment's notice, the only part which is immediately available is the small proportion — now only about 8 per cent — which is made up of notes and coins and the balances which the banks keep with the Bank of England. The reason why these balances rank as cash is very simple. Just as anybody can go to his bank and ask for the money which he has deposited to be paid to him in notes, so the banks can ask the Bank of England for the amount of their deposits in notes. Not only does the Bank of England keep a large supply of notes in reserve, but it can do what nobody else can do: it can print more. In fact it keeps its own printing works for the purpose.

Notes, coins and their balances with the Bank of England are known as the banks' cash reserve. As the name implies, these took the place which gold had previously filled in the monetary system, and became in turn the regulator of credit. Thus the amount of credit-money in the country depended on them, and as long as everybody remembered that they represented gold, all went well. When the Bank of England wished to restrict credit it took steps to reduce the balances which it held for the other banks, the usual method being known as 'open-market operations'. The Bank would sell securities in the market, the purchasers would write cheques on their own banks, and when the Bank received them it would deduct the amounts from the balances. As these balances formed the greater part of the other banks' cash reserves, it was a comparatively simple matter to reduce them whenever it was considered that they were being too free with their credits. It was equally possible to reverse the process and thus enable the banks to expand their credits again.

It is difficult to believe that in their new, non-metallic form the banks' cash reserves would have continued indefinitely to command the respect which had always been accorded to gold. For gold was gold — there was nothing else like it — while figures in a ledger and notes which could be printed overnight belonged to an entirely different order of things; the coins were a minor item, and in any case they were only made of nickel. If it had not been for the war, and the vast increase both in notes and credit which it brought, it is possible that the new cash reserves might still be regulating the supply of credit, but there are good reasons for doubting it. For in addition to the flood of new money in every form, other powerful factors were working to undermine it. First, there was now a new generation of bankers who knew nothing about gold and for whom the words 'cash reserve' therefore failed to command the old respect; and secondly — we will use the words of the Radcliffe Report —'the forces making for expansion of bank advances are very strong'.

As long as the cash reserve in its new form continued to regulate the supply of credit, bankers observed the old '12 per cent rule' by which they held twelve pounds of cash against every hundred pounds of deposits. But when at last the inevitable happened and cash ceased to be the effective regulator, the actual size of the reserve was no longer of great impotance, and in 1946 the figure was reduced to 8 per cent. The Radcliffe Report is perfectly explicit about this. 'There has been no attempt in the post-war period to operate on the banking position by limiting the supply of cash: the banks have always been automatically provided with whatever was necessary to make their cash ratios fit the 8 per cent rule imposed since 1946.'

What, then, took the place of the cash reserve as the regulator of credit? The Radcliffe Report tells us: 'the credit-creating capacity of the banks is limited by the "30 per cent liquid assets convention"'; and again, 'the liquid assets of the joint stock banks are today their effective credit base; an increase in the amount of liquid assets in the banking system may therefore make possible an increase in the banks' lending to the public'. The liquid assets which are now accepted as the regulator of credit are made up as follows: first there is the original 8 per cent of cash; there is approximately the same amount in 'money at call', and the balance, which is usually a little less than half the total, consists of bills discounted, of which about nine tenths are Treasury Bills. 'Treasury Bills have a special significance in that when held by a clearing bank they are "liquid assets" for the purpose of the liquid assets ratio'. But as the banks are free to buy as many Treasury Bills as they can pay for — and that is a great many — it soon became clear that within wide limits they could expand their holdings of liquid assets pretty well at will. 'The management of their 'liquid assets' (minimum 30 per cent in March each year) causes little trouble to the banks. An individual bank has to be prepared to reinforce its liquid assets by selling investments, and it can run down its liquid assets in order to buy investments. The composition of the liquid assets is also managed very easily: it is a purely technical task to be coped with day by day'. Thus the real meaning of the new convention was that for all practical purposes the control of the supply of credit had been transferred to the banks themselves. The last trace of the system of 1844 had indeed disappeared.

What, then, remained to set a limit to the creation of credit-money, with the notes which accompany it, and to prevent the banks flooding the country with money on a scale which had not been seen since the days of the South Sea Bubble? Why, in fact, has inflation not gone even further than it has? At the date when the Radcliffe Committee issued their report the answer to this question was a very simple one: the banks were unable to find any more suitable borrowers. 'The banks remain in this position of feeling that they could comfortably lend more on overdraft if only they could find more credit-worthy customers.' The Report describes all their efforts to find more borrowers by such means as granting credit for exports, building tankers and making personal loans for the purchase of cars and other things. It leaves in fact no room for doubt that the final decision as to how much money we are to have was being left to the banks' customers, the public. It was certainly a strange development. We had travelled a long way from the days when a banker would hardly dare to make another loan before he had checked the amount of gold in his vaults. We had travelled so far that we appeared to have reached the end of the road.

When the Radcliffe Committee issued their report, in August

1959, the Government had already been trying for nearly eight years to restrain the banks. They had begun towards the end of 1951 by raising the Bank Rate and issuing a series of 'hints from headquarters', but these had little effect and early in 1952 they raised the Bank Rate again, this time more sharply. Bank advances now began to decline and in the following year the 'squeeze' was relaxed, whereupon the advances shot forward again. In June 1955 the Chancellor of the Exchequer requested the banks to make 'a positive and significant reduction in their advances', and a year later he took 'the unprecedented step' of summoning the leading bankers to the Treasury and lecturing them in person. In 1956 it was considered safe to give the banks their freedom again, but the rise in advances was so great that in 1957 the squeeze was renewed in an exceptionally severe form, the Bank Rate being raised to 7 per cent. When it was removed in the following year bank advances increased by £382 million. The total increase since 1952 was no less than £586 million.

We have already seen how bank advances tend to perpetuate themselves, and even to increase, for although a customer may not wish to borrow more, if he is unable to meet his half-yearly interest charges they are added to the total of his loan. These half-yearly charges now amount to nearly £90 million and it is estimated that between a third and a half of this sum is added to the total of advances. This is all new money, and in its effect on the economy it only differs from the original loan in that it is put into circulation by the banks — when the loan is eventually repaid — instead of by their customers. Sooner or later these interest charges will be added to the existing volume of purchasing power and will increase the forces making for inflation. Thus the authorities are faced with a situation in which not only are the banks constantly exerting pressure to increase their advances, but the advances already made are often found to be generating a second pressure of their own.

When we described the origin of the Trade Cycle we explained how the banks gave the wheel its first upward turn with their loans, and how the interest charged on them then helped to give it a second one. The Radcliffe Committee remind us that their predecessors the Macmillan Committee preferred

to describe the Cycle as the 'Credit Cycle', which is certainly
more accurate. But whatever name we call it by, it is clearly the
same old enemy which has been plaguing us intermittently for
two hundred and fifty years, and the forces behind it are
still the same.

The Radcliffe Committee paid a great deal of attention to the
problem of limiting the banks' powers to create credit. Their
report points out, for instance, that 'the authorities can impose a
substantial penalty on banks that wish to expand advances by
running down investments ... This is a conceivable way of
deterring the banks from fully satisfying the demand for advances
...'. But the Committee made it clear that they were not very
hopeful that it would be possible to stop the banks before they
had achieved their objective and become 'fully-lent'; they
appeared in fact to be resigned to await the day when the
'successful exertions by the banks to expand advances, if they
approach the position of a generation ago, will help to restore
the power of the authorities'.

After reviewing in great detail the present situation, the
Radcliffe Committee returned to our own starting-point, the
Act of 1844. 'The 1844 legislation, despite all its shortcom-
ings, was one of the pillars of the English monetary system, and
has left its mark on later statutes even until quite recent times.
We are in effect looking for some 1959 successor to this
traditional restriction of the note issue: some statutory assurance,
fitting to the view we have taken as to how the monetary system
works, that a collapse in the value of the pound will not be
allowed to occur'. But they admit that they have not succeeded
in finding what they were looking for and the reasons which
they give for their failure are very interesting. 'It is frequently
suggested,' they say, 'that the solution is to find some up-to-
date close parallel with the restriction of the note issue: some
way of restricting by statute the supply of money.' But the
Committee show a strange reluctance to examine the sources of
the supply, and they prefer to turn their attention to the money
which 'is already there', or as they usually put it, 'the whole
liquidity position'. Their anxiety to prove that it is the money
already in existence which is the cause of the trouble leads them
to make some remarkable statements. For instance: 'Though

we do not regard the supply of money as an unimportant quantity, we view it as only part of the wider structure of liquidity in the economy. It is the whole liquidity position that is relevant to spending decisions, and our interest in the supply of money is due to its significance in the whole liquidity picture.' What matters, it seems, is only the water which is already in the bath: we must concentrate our attention on that rather than on the tap through which it is still pouring in. And again: 'In a highly developed financial system the theoretical difficulties of identifying "the supply of money" cannot be lightly swept aside. Even when they are disregarded, all the haziness of the connection between the supply of money and the level of total demand remains: the haziness that lies in the impossibility of limiting the velocity of circulation'. It is far from clear what these difficulties are, but it appears that the system is considered in some way responsible for them: while as regards the complaint that it is impossible to limit the velocity of circulation, we must point out that the Committee base this conclusion on their study of our monetary history for only eight years, and these happened to be the years when inflation was at its peak. If they had extended their study to cover a longer period they would have found that the velocity of circulation varied with the condition of the currency. For when people see their money losing its value they naturally hasten to spend it as quickly as possible. At the height of inflation in Austria after the First World War, whenever a notice appeared in the banks showing that the exchange rate of the krone had fallen again, people could be seen running to the shops before they had time to put up their prices. But when money is stable, not only is there no urgency to spend it, but people realize that it is worth saving. There is therefore every reason to believe that when we restore confidence in the currency the velocity of circulation will settle down and follow an established pattern.

Towards the end of their chapter on the Influence of Monetary Measures the Committee use words which can only mean that the real obstacles to reform — the factors which defeat all their efforts to find 'some way of restricting by statute the supply of money' — are to be found in the monetary system itself. For what they say is this: 'In addition to the adaptability of the financial habits of the private sector, we cannot assume an absence of ingenuity on the part of a Government determined to spend but circumscribed in its borrowing powers'. If the system had been reformed on the lines suggested by Ricardo neither the private sector, however adaptable it might be, nor the government of the day, however, anxious to spend, would have been in a position to influence the supply of money. If Peel had taken Ricardo's advice, the Radcliffe Committee would have had an easier task.

The Committee finish the chapter on an unmistakable note of disillusion and defeat. 'But no statutory restrictions, no standing machinery, can constitute real protection; the only sure foundation for confidence lies in an informed and understanding public opinion supporting a Government that keeps in balance the various objectives we have discussed in Chapter II'. If this were in truth the last that could be said about our money, we would clearly have little reason left for hope of any kind. For where money is concerned we have never possessed anything which could be described as an informed and understanding public opinion; while as regards the objectives which the Government must keep in balance, it appears that the task might well prove to be beyond the power of any government, however gifted. For the Committee themselves admit that 'there are serious possibilities of conflict between them'. Thus what they are really offering us amounts to this: our only hope of monetary stability depends on the fulfilment of two conditions. First, we must acquire something which does not exist and has in fact never existed; and secondly, our government must be successful in performing a task which the Committee clearly regard without very great confidence. It looks, in fact, as if what we need is not only one miracle, but two.

Faced with a situation of this kind, a government pledged to fight inflation had the choice of two courses. They could either reform the monetary system and eliminate the weaknesses which were at the root of the trouble; or they could keep the system with all its imperfections and hope that by the exercise of constant vigilance and ingenuity they would be successful in restraining the banks and keeping the issue of credit-money within reasonable limits. Unfortunately they chose the second course.

We know the results of the Government's decision only too well, and we have become accustomed to the monotonous sequence of boom and squeeze, in which the booms tend to become shorter and the squeezes longer. Between the squeezes the banks push out their credits as vigorously as ever; in the course of a single year, from May 1959 to May 1960, bank advances rose by no less than £777 million, bringing the total to £3,457 million. This rise forced the Government to recognize that their traditional weapons, higher bank rates and directives to the banks, could no longer be relied on and they therefore produced a new one known as Special Deposits. The banks were now required to transfer 1 per cent of their deposits with the Bank of England to a special account where they would no longer rank as liquid assets which could be used as the base for new loans. As soon as the first sum had been transferred, in June 1960, the banks were ordered to make a second deposit, also of 1 per cent. These two deposits reduced the banks' liquid assets by about £140 million, but they soon replaced the greater part of it by selling £120 million of their investments.

The persistent pressure of the banks to extend their loans, and the counter measures taken by the Government to prevent them, combined to produce a state of affairs which has been described as a 'stop–start–stop' economy; it has also been said that what we are suffering from is an attack of financial hiccups. The general picture is that of a ding-dong unending struggle between 'the authorities' and the banks. Sometimes one side appears to be winning, sometimes the other; the real victims are the non-combatants, who always lose. These are the unfortunate men whose task it is to manage our industries and make plans for their future development. The big and powerful firms are not as a rule seriously affected as they are able to finance their capital expenditure out of their own resources, but thousands of smaller firms, many of them engaged in specialized branches of engineering, have suffered severely from high interest charges and even more from the atmosphere of uncertainty. For uncertainty is the greatest enemy of confidence, enterprise and initiative, and these are the things which we must have if we are to keep ahead—or even abreast—of our competitors in world markets.

The Radcliffe Report warned us more than once what was

happening. 'The light engineering industries have been frustrated in their planning, and the public corporations have had almost equally disheartening experience. That these two should be the 'residuary legatees' for real resources when sharp adjustments were called for is not a comforting thought. It is far removed from the smooth and widespread adjustment sometimes claimed as the virtue of monetary action; this is no gentle hand on the steering wheel that keeps a well-driven car in its right place on the road.' And again: 'It is the very fast-growing companies that are most exposed to the state of financial markets. This is a reminder that restrictive measures aimed through the financial markets are bound to hurt most those parts of British industry that are growing most rapidly, a category that may be presumed to include many of the "progressive elements".' There is therefore no mystery about the failure of our exporting industries to keep abreast of their foreign competitors; it is the inevitable result of the Government's failure to allow them to expand without constant interruptions, and penal rates of interest when they borrow. It would be comforting to think that the men who direct Russian industry were handicapped in the same way, but the available evidence makes it alarmingly clear that they are not.

'We must all be in this export game', says Mr Macmillan. 'There is a very real need to do better.' There certainly is; but it would be easier to feel confident if Mr Macmillan had discovered that what industry needs is not exhortation, but release from the handicap which the restrictive practices of the monetary system are now imposing on it.

In these days of increasingly stern competition nobody who wishes to see this country prosper will question the need of keeping our factories up to date, and with the evidence which is now available it is no longer possible to doubt that the real obstacles to progress are to be found in our antiquated monetary system. If we stand back and consider it objectively we will be compelled to admit that there was never any reason to believe that it would do the job which we expect it to do. It was not designed for the purpose, and for that matter it can hardly be said to have been designed at all. And when we seek to define the principle on which it works, the only accurate description is that they are little more than those of a balance of power between two opposing forces, the 'authorities' and the banks.

What our industries need is a carefully regulated supply of money, neither too little nor too much, and above all not subject to sudden fluctuations. Clearly this should be decided by the experts after a careful assessment of our needs; but although they doubtless make such assessments, the amount of money which is actually available at any moment will probably be found to depend, not on their decisions, but on the state of the tug-of-war between the authorities and the banks. We must therefore face the fact that in its present form our monetary system is not capable of giving the country the service which it needs and which it is entitled to expect. It is even misleading to call it a system: it is a haphazard, hit-and-miss affair which has no place in the modern world. It is in fact a rather disreputable survival from an age when a great many things went on which would not be tolerated today.

Our monetary system is as much a relic of the past as are our winding roads which are another, though far less serious, drag on our efficiency. Like the system, they came into existence piece-meal and without a plan, twisting and turning to suit the wishes of the local land owners. They may have served their purpose well enough in the leisurely days of horse traffic, but their endless bends and corners can now reduce the speed of modern cars to little more than that of stage coaches. The modern, progressive industries on which our future depends can be compared to the new powerful cars which are only allowed to reach their full performance for a few minutes at a time: an occasional brief spurt, and the driver has to apply the brakes again. If he wants a road where he can travel mile after mile at a steady speed with his foot on the accelerator, he must go to the M1. That is indeed a modern road, built for modern cars and modern speeds. What we need now is a modern monetary system which will make it possible for our industries to show what they too can do when they are given a chance.

10

A TRIBUTE TO PROFESSOR FREDERICK SODDY

Some time after his death in September 1956 I was invited to give the Soddy Memorial Lecture as a tribute to his contribution to economic and monetary reform. I welcomed this opportunity to pay a sincere tribute to a man who was both a personal friend and one from whom I learned a great deal about money and its place in a modern economy. I think it worth including this tribute here, particularly in view of the failure to give sufficient recognition to his unique contribution in the world of science.

SODDY MEMORIAL LECTURE

To do real justice to the contribution made by Frederick Soddy in the sphere of economic and monetary policy would necessitate writing a substantial volume. I have been asked to undertake this task in the course of one necessarily brief lecture and I can only plead that this is virtually an impossibility. I can only touch on the contribution which Soddy made and hope as a result to stimulate further study and research into the clear-sighted thinking which he made available on this highly controversial and somewhat difficult subject.

His unique position in the scientific world had made Soddy fully aware of the fact that, largely through the medium of science and technological advance, the problems which had confronted humanity in past ages, the problem of producing sufficient wealth, had very largely been solved. In writing of the failure of money to fulfil its proper role as the means of ensuring that the benefits of science and technology should be passed on to the human race, Soddy wrote of

92

a monstrous cancer invading the heart of the nation and turning to evil the good that might reasonably have been expected to follow the solution of the problem of wealth production.

Although much has changed in the years since the words quoted were written, the effects of the monetary system still poison human relationships both nationally and internationally. We have developed an acquisitive society based on the love of money and we still grope for the solution to our problems in spite of the fact that, with his truly scientific analysis, Soddy signposted the direction we should take to solve our problems.

So many of the difficulties which arise in our modern society, the difficulties between employer and worker, the restrictive practices which are still rife, the strikes, go-slows and such things, continue because we have failed to bring the ordinary facts regarding economics and money to ordinary people. This arises from our failure to introduce a sane method of distribution by adopting a scientific monetary mechanism. The same is true of the deteriorating relationships between nations. A sane system of payments between nations in line with the needs of the second half of the twentieth century would do much to restore good-neighbour relations between the peoples of the world.

It is significant, I suggest, that Professor Soddy's book, perhaps his most important economic work, entitled *Wealth, Virtual Wealth and Debt*, has recently been republished by an American publisher in the United States. Written in 1926, this book certainly repays study even though it was first published thirty-five years ago. This cannot be said of all the economic textbooks published in the 1920s!

Frederick Soddy's achievements in the world of science certainly entitle him to a place with the really great men of our time. Equally, his contribution to sane economics will stand the test of time, and he will one day be recognised as one of the few courageous and disinterested men, who, casting personal recognition on one side, carried on a ceaseless fight against the preposterous humbug of finance. Unfortunately, it was his forthright and uncompromising advocacy of reform of the monetary system which militated against proper recognition being given to his scientific achievements in his own lifetime, except among the few who really knew.

In the 1930s we used to discuss what we called the 'conspiracy of silence' which surrounded the whole sphere of monetary policy in the years between the wars. Unfortunately, this still applies today, even though many of the claims we then made are now freely admitted by orthodox economists. One can understand Soddy's anger when it is realised that persistent adherence to the then orthodox deflationary monetary policy which was accepted after the First World War was directly responsible for the unemployment and suffering of those years and led inevitably to the Second World War. I do not think it an exaggeration to say that had Frederick Soddy's economic views been listened to and his ideas acted upon, instead of being ignored, the Second World War could have been avoided with all its destruction and loss of life.

It was my privilege to be associated with Soddy during the period from 1930 until his death. We had a number of able and sincere colleagues, like Arthur Kitson, the doyen of monetary reformers to whom Soddy paid tribute as being the man who first drew his attention to monetary problems, Vincent Vickers, a former director of the Bank of England, Lord Sempill, Lord Northbourne, Sir Reginald Rowe and many others formed a significant group of people who really understood the true implications of the money question. Together, we formed the Economic Reform Club and Institute (now merged with the Economic Research Council). This institute, which did a great deal of good work in the years from 1936 was proud to have Frederick Soddy as one of its Vice-Presidents for the whole period of its existence. While we recognised that he was not one of the easiest men to work with, we were proud to be associated with him in so many of our endeavours. In those days we were all dismissed rather contemptuously as 'monetary cranks'. I well remember the phrase used by the late Governor of the Bank of England, Montagu Norman, who said on one occasion 'The dogs may bark but the caravan marches on'. The dogs are still barking!

As everyone who came into close association with Soddy

soon found out, he was a born fighter who particularly despised hypocricy and stupidity. He found both of these extremely nauseating and in the sphere of monetary policy he found plenty of both. Soddy found it particularly hard to stomach the falsity of the system which permitted book entries to rank as money. He is perhaps best known in the monetary reform world for his £ for £ scheme, of which he was the originator. This idea was later advocated by Professor Irving Fisher in the United States in his book entitled *100% Money*. Under this system the commercial banks would be required to hold actual notes to the total value of their deposits, instead of holding only 8 per cent of cash as the basis on which they are permitted to create credit.

It is only comparatively recently that the banks have admitted they can and do create and destroy credit. As Soddy commented, 'if some people are to be allowed to issue and destroy money, all the others may as well give up at once any idea of economic independence or freedom, and hire themselves out to those who have this power at the best terms they can'.

It appears today that too many able people have found it necessary to do just this. The results are plain to see, for in both the internal and the international sphere, conditions are chaotic. They will only get worse until there are enough men and women with the calibre of Frederick Soddy, able and willing to challenge the power of money without fear of the consequences. When this happens, we can begin to put our affairs in order.

Soddy's views on the creation of money are summarised in his statement that

> the State itself should issue genuine money at a rate which will keep the average price of goods or the price index constant from one century to another.

At a time when the majority of monetary reformers were taking a somewhat superficial view that all that was needed to remedy the deflation of the 1920s and 1930s was the issue of more money, Soddy was pointing out that until something had been produced and was available for sale, the issue of new money was unjustified and the result was bound to be inflationary. In other words, new money is only needed when there are more goods and services available. Until this new wealth exists the creation of new money merely dilutes the value of the existing money.

The truth of this view was well demonstrated after the Second World War. The authorities, who had resolutely refused to countenance the creation of more money when this was completely justified, now became convinced that the de-flation of the inter-war years was both unnecessary and harmful. So they decided to go in for thorough-going inflation. During the years 1938–57 the monetary authorities allowed the amount of money in circulation to increase three and a half times. In this same period gross national production increased by about 30 per cent. The value of money depreciated from 20/- in 1938 to 6/6d in 1957. The purchasing power of the £ was depreciated by two-thirds.

This was just as much a policy of self-deception as was the deflation of the inter-war years. In the 1920s we deceived our-selves into thinking we were poor when we were comparatively rich. The result was unemployment and misery, when if we had used the resources available, we could have had a high standard of living. Equally, after 1945, we deceived ourselves into believing that we were rich when we were comparatively poor. Our blood and treasure had been poured out to fight a war, yet it was just at this time that we decided that we could all have much more money. Such self-deception is only possible when the majority of people do not understand money, and it makes incomprehensible the refusal of the authorities to take notice of the vitally important contribution made on this subject by Frederick Soddy.

'The Banks,' said Soddy 'have usurped the prerogative of the Crown with regard to the issue of money and corrupted the purpose of money from that of an exchange medium to that of an interest-bearing debt, but the real evil is that we now have a concertina instead of a currency.' How true this is has been clearly demonstrated by the post-war years:

It is clear that the issue and withdrawal of money should be re-stored to the nation for the general good and should entirely cease from providing a source of livelihood to private corporations. Money should not bear interest because of its existence, but only when genuinely lent by an owner who gives it up to the borrower.

This statement of Soddy's challenges the whole concept of money as we now know it, and there are powerful forces who are quite determined that these ideas shall never be implemented. Yet the acceptance of this rule would clear the way for an honest approach to money both internally and internationally and would undoubtedly benefit all concerned in the long run.

'Clearly, the profits of the issue of money should belong to the Community.' wrote Soddy. Here again he challenges one of the sacred cows of the present system. It is fantastic that the sovereign government of this country when it requires new money to finance national projects should have to 'borrow' this from the banking system. This is a matter to which we have returned time and time again. I recall a Memorandum which twenty-one of us, including Soddy, forwarded in 1939 to the then Chancellor of the Exchequer. In his reply Sir John Simon noted that it was suggested that the Government should assume control of the financial system and obtain whatever funds the banks may lend to it free of interest. He commented that these far-reaching proposals are not new and he did not think that a discussion with a deputation would be likely to throw any new light on them.

Since that date the Bank of England has been nationalised, but the government continues to 'borrow' from the banking system as heretofore. Although we did not succeed at the beginning of the war in 1939 in getting interest-free money issued to finance the war, we did succeed in our campaign to bring down the Bank Rate. This meant that interest rates were reduced, so that the last war was financed on borrowing at 3½ per cent instead of 5 per cent. The saving to the nation in interest charges was colossal. The effect of increasing rates of interest on the cost of borrowing is illustrated by a statement made in the House of Commons by the Chancellor of the Exchequer. He was replying to a question about the eventual cost of a Council House costing £1600 to build after repayment over 60 years now that rates of interest had been raised to 6⅛ per cent.

The Chancellor gave the reply that the total amount repayable would be £6042.

In 1957 we had the Radcliffe Committee set up to inquire into the working of the monetary and credit system and to make recommendations. Its report was published in 1959 and its chief value lies in the fact that we now have an authoritative account of the working of the present system, stripped of the mystery which formerly shrouded its operations. It is now clear where money comes from, how and by whom it is created. Soddy and others who were dismissed as 'cranks' for saying that the commercial banks had the power to create and destroy money are now completely vindicated. As I can claim to have played a considerable part in the activities which led to the Radcliffe Committee being set up, I feel that I am entitled to express disappointment at their failure to make any worthwhile proposals for reform of the system which they so adequately describe in their report. But perhaps that was too much to hope for.

It was also in 1957 that our hopes were raised when Mr Peter Thorneycroft, then Chancellor of the Exchequer, made use of a favourite phrase of Soddy's—'Honest Money'. Unfortunately, when he spoke of Honest Money he did not mean acceptance of Soddy's views, though at long last there was a belated recognition that to create more and more money without a corresponding increase in wealth to consume was simply to dilute the value of existing money. Since then, however, we have had the melancholy picture of the 'stop–go' economy. The banks' ability to create new credit in times of expansion knows virtually no limit. This leads to the threat of inflation which gets out of hand. The authorities take steps to curb inflation by the imposition of a credit squeeze and high bank rate. These have the effect of stifling production and we have the threat of recession.

This is how Mr Peter Thorneycroft himself described the monetary system as seen from Ministerial level in the Treasury:

> It appeared like an antiquated pumping machine, creaking and groaning, leaking idly at all the main valves, but still desperately

attempting to keep down the level of water in the mine. There was quite a lot of water in the mine at that time and more was seeping in.

Perhaps he had been reading Professor Soddy after all!

The present Chancellor is now talking about introducing some kind of planning body. Unfortunately, here again he appears to ignore the basis of Soddy's view, which is that consumption needs planning scientifically by a body charged with the maintenance of a stable price level. The truth is that following the Radcliffe Report the authorities seem to have despaired of making monetary policy do the job it is supposed to do and are seeking alternatives which can only mean greater regimentation and loss of freedom by the individual. It is sad to see the views of Frederick Soddy still ignored when the need for understanding of his scientific approach is more than ever needed.

In the realm of international trade, Soddy contented himself with recommendations as to the proper place of gold which would be used as a commodity for international transactions, useful in adjusting the balance of trade between nations. He wanted gold dethroned from a controlling position, but recognised that it still had a place to fill. He relied mainly on his proposals for reform in the internal sphere to remedy the external position, and there is no doubt that if his ideas had been applied, the international situation would have been greatly ameliorated. He once told me that he was very sympathetic to the views which I had supported for reform in the international sphere and that these dovetailed perfectly into his own internal proposals.

In assessing the contributions made by Frederick Soddy to modern thought on money it is obvious that considerable advances have been made. The Radcliffe Committee on credit and currency admits most of the case made by Soddy about the creation of money and the way the system works. But much remains to be done and the time is growing short. If we are not careful we shall find that our sovereign control of money which still remains at Westminster will no longer reside there, but will have been passed on to even less accessible authority. In the *Daily Telegraph* Sir John Lomax in a letter makes this point with clarity. Having referred to the continued debasement of the £ sterling and the failure of Parliament to take remedial action, he wrote:

> our voice in foreign affairs—even where our vital interests lie—is muted to a nervous whisper lest we should offend foreign countries with gold reserves enough to land us in another sterling crisis.

On the other hand, we have Lord Cromer, making his first important speech as Governor of the Bank of England, telling an audience of bankers and merchants that 'Increases in money profits or money incomes only represented increases in real wealth if the increased money was matched by an equivalent increase in goods and services. Otherwise the increase in money be it in profits or incomes, merely meant paying more money for the same goods. This', declared Lord Cromer, 'cannot be widely enough understood.' Compare this with Soddy's view that new money should only be created when there are more goods and services available and you see that some advance towards economic enlightenment has been made. There is also the fact that small communities—the Isle of Man, Jersey and Guernsey—have all taken steps to use their ancient privilege of printing their own money and using this as a means of providing themselves with a debt-free and interest-free issue of currency which can enable them to put unused resources to work.

Only when the real function of money is properly understood, only when it is realised that money is not wealth itself, and we cease to allow it to bear a rate of interest merely because of its existence, but only when genuinely lent by an owner who gives up its use to a borrower, shall we be able to destroy the power of money, that 'monstrous cancer invading the heart of the nation'. Then at last we should be able to go forward and use the bountiful resources made possible by the work of the scientist and technologist to the benefit of the entire human race. When that day comes, Frederick Soddy will surely be recognised as one of the architects of the New Age.

11

RHODESIAN INTERLUDE

Some time in 1962 I received a letter from the Duke of Montrose, known in Rhodesia as Lord Graham, a long-standing member of the Economic Reform Club, who farmed in Rhodesia. He asked if there was any possibility of my paying a visit to Rhodesia to discuss monetary and economic policy with a group which had been formed to study these matters. He said that in Southern Rhodesia, as it was then called, they had vast potential wealth allied to a large population with a low standard of living. 'We would like you to come and visit us and discuss what could be done to stimulate the economy of this territory so that we can not only benefit ourselves but the whole community by the development of the wealth which undoubtedly exists here.'

Needless to say, I was very attracted by this proposal, but with a very heavy lecture programme as well as other activities it was not until May 1963 that I was able to make arrangements to visit Rhodesia. In the interim an interesting event had taken place. The group that had invited me had, in the meantime, become the Government. This put my visit on a very different footing, and when I arrived in Rhodesia the doors opened in every direction. I found it possible to meet most of the leading people in the community—bankers, industrialists, government officials and civil servants as well as farmers and agricultural experts. It was a pleasant experience to receive VIP treatment for a change!

The impression I gained from my conversations and visits to many parts of the country completely confirmed the view that there was a vast reservoir of potential wealth waiting development. Although I was only in the country from 8 May until 4 June I managed to meet a great many people, including the tribal chiefs who were gathering in Salisbury at that time. After ten days spent mainly in interviews in Salisbury I had a meeting with the top civil servants, when the main topic was how best to develop the economy. Following this meeting I drafted a document setting out my provisional findings and this paper was widely circulated. Following this I had a meeting with the Cabinet at one of their informal discussions. To them I put two major points:

(1)   That successful economic development depended on the full use of resources of manpower and skills which must be contributed from all sections of the community; and
(2)   That equally it meant that all sectors of the community must benefit from the resultant increased wealth. Any attempt to restrict this to the white population would mean that the additional wealth created could not be consumed and recession would result.

Both points were accepted without quibble.

One thing that encouraged me was that the then Prime Minister, Winston Field, told me that he was well aware of my writings on economic and monetary affairs which he had studied over many years as a result of the formation of the Southern Rhodesian Branch of the Economic Reform Club in the pre-war years.

After the first ten days I spent the rest of my time in an extensive tour of the country, and was most impressed by all I saw, particularly the development of the Hippo Valley Estates. In an area which only five years before had no population to speak of, there were now 9000 Africans and 300 Europeans fully employed.

A rather amusing incident occurred on the way to the Hippo Valley from Fort Victoria. I reported at the airfield at the crack of dawn for the flight, which went first to the Triangle Estate, then on to the Hippo Valley. On arrival I was assured that the plane was fully booked, there were no seats available. A hasty conference took place with some officials whereupon I was told I should fly as co-pilot.

Needless to say I was a bit nervous when I found myself

confronted with the controls but the pilot assured me that, provided I did not touch anything, all would be well.

As we came in to land the pilot leant out of the small aircraft and banged vigorously on the side of the plane. After this performance had been repeated several times I asked why he was doing this. He explained, 'The landing wheels are jammed and if I bang hard enough they will probably free themselves'. 'What if they don't?' I hesitantly asked. 'Oh,' said the pilot, 'then I have to zoom down and then zoom up again, that usually does the trick.' Needless to say, we landed without incident.

The difference in approach to work by the black Africans was explained to me by one of the works managers. He said that monetary incentives scarcely existed among the majority of those employed. Different incentives were required, and chief among these was increased leisure. So they had instituted a method by which the work which should be completed in a week was carefully estimated and the workers told that this amount had to be completed; then they would be free to indulge in their own pursuits. The result, the work was completed in 3 or 4 days and the rest of the time was spent fishing or on some similar pleasant activity. None of them suffered from ulcers! It seemed a rather civilised approach to me, well understood by both employer and worker.

All depended on the provision of water and irrigation. I subsequently submitted a Memorandum to Ian Smith, then the Minister of Treasury, in which I dealt with this and other relevant matters. As this Memorandum contains some of my thinking on economic and monetary matters the following quotation may be of interest:

'I came away convinced that given the right economic and financial policies a significant rate of growth could be achieved in a relatively short period. A preliminary estimate of the rate of growth of 10 per cent per annum has been made, but I believe this to be on the conservative side, given the vast potential which became increasingly evident as I travelled round the country.

The kind of development which seemed to me to be the best for the country stems from the provision of water for irrigation, also the provision of power, making possible the planting and growing of suitable crops. Arising from this, the provision of plant and factories for processing and the ancillary industrial growth which stems from the basis of a thriving and prosperous agriculture. This would, to some extent, attract labour to areas needing population and would tend to reverse the drift of man-power to the existing towns. Stimulation of secondary industries would arise from the demand created by the newly developing areas.

An essential element in initiating such policies is confidence and this necessitates a clearer understanding by the community of the basic facts governing the creation and issue of credit and currency.

Experience in the United Kingdom

One of the major errors of policy in the United Kingdom in recent years has, in my view, been the failure to establish any realistic discipline in the growth of effective demand. Thus during a period of expansion the latent demands of consumers both for capital goods and consumer goods had been allowed to grow at an unrealistic rate. This arises because during a period of expansion there is virtually no effective limit on the amount of new money which can be put into circulation. The Radcliffe Report on Credit and Currency made this clear. It said, 'spending is not limited by the amount of money in existence but it is related to the amount of money people think they can get hold of'. This emphasises the vital psychological aspect of monetary policy and demonstrates the need for discipline in the sphere of currency and credit creation. Having removed the discipline of control through the operation of the gold standard no satisfactory regulator has been established under a 'managed currency' system.

The role of money in this 'managed currency' era must be re-examined. It will be found that during the last fifty years there has been a major change in the role of money. At the beginning of the century it was still backed by something of intrinsic value—gold. The Central Bank was responsible for ensuring that the bank-note of a given denomination could be converted by the bearer into a constant weight of gold. When Britain went off the gold standard this provision no longer applied and she went on to a 'managed currency'. Under this the regulating mechanism, gold, had been removed but no adequate regulator was introduced to take its place.

Money and Goods

To a very large extent the false illusion that money itself is of instrinsic value has been maintained. This false view must give

(*Above*) The author's birth certificate, showing the two dates of birth as 13 and 26 July 1906. (*Below*) The author's parents in Warsaw (1907)

(*Above*) Early days in Rovno with family and friends. (*Below*)
Passport for travelling in Russia in 1909

(*Above*) The author in his office at 26 Grosvenor Place
(1937). (*Below*) Vincent Cartwright Vickers (1939)

Parliamentary candidate (1945)

Sir Ian MacTaggart

Patrick de Laszlo

Damon de Laszlo

The author in his later years

place to the realisation that the real backing for money and credit today is the goods and the services available for consumption by the community. This fact has been constantly ignored when dealing with the problem of both inflation and deflation. In the United Kingdom between the years 1938 and 1957, the amount of money in circulation increased three and a half times. In the same period gross national production increased by about only one-third. The value of the pound sterling deteriorated from 20/- in 1938 to 6/6*d* in 1957. We now require three £1 notes to buy what one £1 note bought in 1938. A solution to this problem can be found by relating the amount of money in circulation as purchasing power, to the quantity of goods and services available for consumption.

Recent experience has also shown that it is not only the quantity of money but also the velocity of circulation which must be taken into account. It is clear that the turnover of money may vary considerably and that these variations intensify the effect of the quantity of money in either direction. Generally speaking, more money in circulation, if not related to an increase in production, will cause people to spend faster. Less money will reduce the velocity of circulation. Moreover rising prices cause stockpiling and buying ahead. Falling prices result in running down stocks and cancellation of orders.

These fluctuations in the velocity of circulation accentuate inflationary and deflationary trends. If reasonable stability in the economy could be maintained the velocity of circulation would tend to settle down to an established pattern. The conclusion I draw from the foregoing is that some way is needed to equate the demands for goods and services to the available supply. It is accepted that the result of having too little money in circulaton is a fall in the price level and appreciation in the value of money. This is clearly indicated by the experience in the United Kingdom during the deflationary era of the 1920s. Recent experience shows that when there is too much money in circulation prices rise and money deteriorates in value. This surely gives a clue to the most effective regulator—the index of the general price level. This should be based on a cost-of-living index embracing a very wide selection of goods and services. If a determined attempt were made to maintain the stability of the price index, tendencies towards both inflation and deflation could be largely eliminated.

This leads to the need for a new authority to implement this policy. An authority that would be answerable to Parliament but removed as far as possible from interference from party and political considerations. The task would be to ensure that the total effective demand for goods and services was maintained at the highest possible level compatible with the stability of the internal general price level.

The main obstacle to development was clearly the lack of adequate finance at rates of interest which made the projects under consideration financially viable.

The view that the necessary finance could only come from sources outside the country and that failing the provision of overseas investment nothing could be done, was constantly challenged by those with whom I discussed matters. This was a source of encouragement to me in putting forward the view that so long as indigenous resources of material and man-power were utilized there was no good reason why the needed capital should not, to some extent, be generated by the Southern Rhodesian Government as a means of setting unused resources in motion.

This view was scarcely challenged, though banking representatives were, somewhat naturally, rather more cautious as to the extent to which this could be done. As a general proposition, an initiative by the Southern Rhodesian Government along these lines would find a ready acceptance among those most concerned. This favourable climate of opinion provides an excellent background for the adoption of modern techniques of providing finance while maintaining the essential confidence which is vital to the success of such policies.

It was interesting to see that the Rhodesian Ministry of Agriculture was devoting quite a lot of effort in trying to educate the black Africans to become cash-crop instead of subsistence farmers. Left to their own devices, the black farmer tended to grow a few mealies, enough to keep his own family from starving, but did little to provide food for the market. I was impressed by what I saw in the attempt to reverse this trend, although it was obvious that it was a long-term project, requiring much patience and persuasion.

It was this kind of development which encouraged me to believe that, given time, Rhodesia could find its way to a more equal society which would be based on the valuable contribution made by both the white and black population. A more prosperous society would inevitably bring up the standard of living of the less favoured black population. In fact, as I said to the Rhodesian Cabinet, prosperity depended on this being given a high priority as the wealth produced increased.

It is a great tragedy that, as a result of the fighting over so many years, the present situation in Zimbabwe, as Rhodesia is now called, is one of threatened famine unless much more aid is provided from outside the country. It may have been a mistake for the Rhodesian Front Government to have declared UDI in 1965, but such an action was understandable in view of the intense exasperation felt on all sides as a result of the policies of successive British governments. This was made very evident by all those I discussed with during my visit, which was, of course, before UDI.

It is difficult to understand why, when independence was conferred on the two other territories comprising the Federation of Rhodesia and Nyasaland, now Zambia and Malawi, the same treatment was not meted out to Southern Rhodesia, which had never been ruled by Westminster, had appointed her own High Commissioners and provided her own armed forces as well as attending Commonwealth Conferences. To say nothing of the splendid contribution Rhodesians had made in the last war.

However, one can only hope that under the leadership of Robert Mugabe, who at the time of writing, seems to realise how much he depends on white agriculture, is seeking to unify the nation under black leadership. The wealth is there and can still be exploited to give a high standard of living to all citizens, black and white, if right policies are followed.

It is all the more disturbing, therefore, to read reports in the press that political opponents of Mr Mugabe have alleged that between 20,000 and 30,000 have been killed in an eighteen-month 'reign of terror' by Government forces in Matabeleland. Moreover, the Rev Ndabaningi Sithole, the founder of the Zimbabwe African National Union Party, is on record as saying 'All political opposition is now being crushed and I expect Mr Mugabe to set up his one-party state by the middle of this year. It will be an instrument of tyranny and dictatorship.'

This makes depressing reading when I recall that I was able to travel the length and breadth of Rhodesia under the Premiership of Mr Winston Field without sensing any hostility or feeling of danger.

When I attended a meeting of the tribal chiefs in Salisbury, far from feeling any sense of hostility, there was a marked cordiality between white politicians and black chiefs. The main subject under discussion was how to improve agricultural production. Even at the University, where there was some opposition to government policies, there was no hint of the kind of bloodshed that has afflicted the country in subsequent years.

12

THE ECONOMIC RESEARCH COUNCIL

In addition to the Research Studies and other publications which the Council has produced over the years, it has, since its inception, invited leading politicians, industrialists, economists and others to speak to members and their guests at dinner meetings. These originated with Sir John Mactaggart, when he was Chairman in the early days. He very generously provided the Council with offices at 55 Park Lane, and he also was host at a number of informal meetings held in the Angus Room in the same building. Guests were first entertained in the restaurant and then adjourned to the meeting. The average attendance was about 25–30 members. Among those who spoke at these early gatherings were Hugh Gaitskell, Professor Hawtrey, Sir Roy Harrod, Harold Wincott of the *Financial Times* and W. Manning Dacey.

When I took over as Honorary Secretary in 1954 the membership of the Council stood at about 70, paying an annual subscription of five shillings. As the two covenants provided by Sir John Mactaggart and Wilfrid Hill had come to an end it was obviously necessary to find other sources of finance if the Council was to continue to function. It thus became essential to build up the membership and so to establish an income sufficient to finance the work entailed. As part of this process we began organising dinner meetings on a more ambitious level. St Ermin's Hotel in Westminster provided an excellent venue and the many eminent speakers* drew increasingly larger audiences. The two guest speakers who commanded the biggest audience (over 200) were Enoch Powell, who spoke on 'Inflation' and also on 'Economic Measures', and Professor (now Lord)

---

* For a fuller list see Appendix II.

Kaldor, who spoke on 'Investment Incentives'. When Reginald Maudling was Chancellor of the Exchequer his subject was 'Full Employment and Economic Stability'. Shortly afterwards James Callaghan gave a talk on 'Prospects for 1964'. At this time Mr Callaghan was studying economic questions to enable him to take over as Chancellor of the Exchequer if and when the next Labour government was returned. He was thus able to talk much more freely than Mr Maudling, who was somewhat inhibited by his Treasury responsibility. Following his address I heard one life-long Tory say 'if that speech indicated Labour policy I would vote Labour'!

It has become increasingly obvious that whatever views on changes of policy a new Chancellor might have on taking office, he is likely to be overwhelmed by the orthodox Treasury approach. It would take a most unusual politician to resist this and thus to succeed in injecting new policies against the orthodoxies of the Treasury in the sphere of financial policy.

Lord Reith was an outstanding contributor to our series of dinner meetings. Several members of the Thatcher Government, including Sir Geoffrey Howe, John Biffen, Sir Keith Joseph, Leon Brittan and Viscount Trenchard, have spoken to us, mainly when they were in Opposition.

In spite of the great care taken in the arrangements for these occasions, there have been one or two crises arising from the uncertainty of political life. On one occasion Denis Healey had agreed to speak and during the morning of the dinner he telephoned to say that he had to speak in a debate at short notice and could not be with us. I asked him to suggest an alternative speaker from the Labour benches and he suggested Brian Walden as one of the best speakers on the Labour side. Fortunately he was able to accept and gave us an outstanding address. On another occasion we had invited Rhodes Boyson to speak and he also phoned at very short notice to say that he would be detained at the House and could not come. On this occasion I volunteered to speak. This sticks in my mind because, at that time I was using contact lenses. At the critical moment they fell out and everything was a blur. I could neither see my rough notes or the audience. Somehow, I managed to talk for about 40 minutes and from all accounts the evening went very well.

On another occasion when John Moore, MP was due to talk on energy policy he was sent overseas at short notice on an urgent mission for the Prime Minister. Damon de Laszlo, Chairman of the Council, very ably led a discussion on the subject. However, considering the large number of dinners, several at the House of Lords, which the Council has arranged, things have gone very smoothly and members seem very appreciative of the opportunity to meet and hear leading figures in the sphere of finance and economics. Proof of this is the fact that the membership now varies between 500 and 600. Perhaps the most intriguing development was the contretemps which followed the dinner when Professor Kaldor spoke. This really was a 'storm in a teacup'.

In the latter part of 1965 the Economic Research Council had its attention drawn to the fact that a large number of the smaller Close Companies, not to mention accountants and solicitors, were under the impression that under the Finance Act of 1965 a Close Company would not only have to pay Corporation Tax but would also be obliged to pay Income Tax on undistributed profits unless it distributed at least 60 per cent.

The result of this, we learned, was that many manufacturing companies who rely on undistributed profits to pay for capital expansion were cutting back their expansion programmes, which we believed was contrary to the national interest.

It so happened that Professor Kaldor, at the time a Government adviser, had agreed to address a meeting of the ERC. This was cleared by an old friend, Niall MacDermot, then the Financial Secretary to the Treasury. Professor Kaldor came to lunch with Patrick de Laszlo and myself before the meeting at which Professor Kaldor was to speak, to discuss arrangements for the occasion. During conversation the question was raised about Close Company taxation and the generally held belief referred to above.

Professor Kaldor said that if this was generally believed it was most unfortunate, and should be dispelled, since he was sure that it had never been the intention of the Chancellor to compel Close Companies to distribute profits required for the legitimate expansion of the business. He then suggested that, though it had been agreed that his address to the ERC and any subsequent debate on the address should be 'off the record', it might, nevertheless, be a convenient opportunity to dispel mis-understanding about this matter if, at the end of his address, the Chairman asked a pre-arranged question about this point to which Professor Kaldor could give a formal answer on the basis that both question and answer would not be 'off the record', and so could be reported in the press.

Professor Kaldor kindly undertook to seek permission from the appropriate authority for this to be done and so, in due course, he made the following pre-arranged statement at our dinner in February 1966:

> I can give you a far reaching and explicit assurance on the point that *nobody in the Government* either on the political side or on the official side *or in the Inland Revenue has any intention to enforce the sections of the Finance Act 1965 on close companies relating to distribution in such a manner as to cause a penny of tax to be paid in cases where money has not been distributed by a close company in order to plough it back into the business.*

The question and answer given by Professor Kaldor were duly reported in the press though, in accordance with the agree-ment, no report was given of the address or subsequent dis-cussion. It aroused little interest at the time.

However, Mr Robin Turton (now Lord Tranmire) was interested, and on 3 May 1966 he asked the Chancellor of the Exchequer whether it was with his authority that Professor Kaldor stated to the Economic Research Council that cash ear-marked by close companies for expansion will not be taxed under the provisions of the Finance Act, 1965.

The Chancellor of the Exchequer answered 'Yes, Sir', and also referred to statements on this matter made during the debate on the Finance Bill on 21 June 1965.

We then learned that during the following twelve months there appeared to be a number of cases in which Close Companies had disclosed in their annual accounts that they had retained more than 60 per cent of their net profits (after Corporation Tax) and had used the money wholly for legitimate expansion of the business. Nevertheless, the Inland Revenue had written letters to the representatives of these companies drawing attention to the 'shortfall', with the implication that unless a distribution was made the company might lay itself open to a claim for Income Tax, and it was understood that in a number of cases auditors had advised their clients to make an additional distribution in order to appease the Inland Revenue.

A typical example is a small business which in 1966 earned a profit of less than £1000. The accounts showed that the company could not distribute any of this profit because the whole of it had been used to finance an increase in debtors and in stock. The Inland Revenue wrote to the auditors as follows:

> I have reviewed these accounts in connection with the provisions of Section 77, Finance Act, 1965, and in my opinion unless a further distribution is made in respect of this accounting period a shortfall will arise.

We felt that though the Chancellor of the Exchequer appeared to have made the matter absolutely clear by his answer in May 1966, the position was still not fully understood by some of the smaller companies; by their financial advisers or even by the staff of the Inland Revenue.

Accordingly, we explained our misgivings to Mr Robin Turton and Mr John Smith, MP, who kindly undertook to clarify the matter again by putting down further questions to the point. Several MPs sought assurances from the Treasury that the explicit and authoritative statement given by the Government in 1966 would be made abundantly clear to all Inspectors of Taxes. They were assured by the spokesman for the Treasury, Mr Diamond, that all Tax Inspectors had been advised.

We felt that as the position had been so fully and unequivocally dealt with by the Government, it would serve a useful purpose for Close Companies if the facts could be clearly reported in the press. Although the question was related to the Finance Bill, 1965, the press treated the matter as being of current concern, and this was just before the Budget of 1966. Consequently it appeared as if it was a Budget leak, and the Chancellor of the Exchequer, James Callaghan, actually took the unusual step of replying to a Question on Budget Day to put the matter right.

The whole matter was really 'a storm in a teacup' but it did show the value of an organisation like the ERC in getting clarification on a matter of considerable importance to smaller companies.

Another worthwhile activity which the Council has promoted over the years has been the publication of 'Occasional Papers' on a large variety of topics. These papers are, in the main, submitted by individual members of the Council who have a particular interest in some specialised subject or aspect of the economy. These papers are first examined by a Publications Committee, who give them careful study. If finally approved they are circulated to those members who are entitled to receive them. A feature of this development is that after the papers have been circulated, a discussion meeting is arranged at which the author of the paper has the opportunity to meet those members who have an interest in the subject of the paper.

In 1965 Professor Sargant Florence contributed a paper on the subject of 'The Public Cost of Large Families'. This was one of the early contributions and aroused a lot of interest. Professor Florence commented: 'This form of debate upon a written statement read as homework beforehand is particularly useful for informing and forming public opinion.'

During the years 1964 to 1970 the Council organised some very successful Study Lecture series. These were intended mainly for economists and business executives and were available as a postal course for those unable to attend the lectures. In 1964 the first of a series of five lectures was under the title 'The British Economy—the next ten years'. In 1965 the subject was 'The Technological Revolution'. As a result of suggestions from members of the Council attention was then turned to more specific subjects, and in 1967 the title was 'Business

Economics'. This was followed in 1968 with 'Taxation Economics' and in 1970 by 'Employment Economics', issued as a postal course only. These lectures were arranged by a member of the Executive Committee, Martin Cadman, who edited both 'Business Economics' and 'Taxation Economics' as textbooks, published by Macmillan.

In June 1965 publication of *Economic Digest* ceased, owing to falling circulation. However, as a result of funds made available through Antony Fisher, the Council was able to launch a new journal entitled *Economic Age*. This was under the editorship of Dennis Thomas, with myself as Managing Editor. We managed to keep this going with some success for two years, but we failed to attract sufficient advertising revenue to enable the journal to continue. It was taken over by the quarterly journal *Twentieth Century*.

The years 1968 to 1970 were a particularly fruitful period for the Council, for during this period the Programme for National Recovery was launched. This is the subject of the next chapter. Also in 1970 Lord Beeching became President, an appointment he held until 1985, when he died. We owe him a great debt for his support for these years, as well as to the former President, Professor Sargant Florence.

The Council now publishes a much more modest quarterly journal entitled *Britain & Overseas*. I inherited this from the now-defunct Commonwealth Industries Association, of which I was Director and Editor for many years. When the journal was adopted as a bi-monthly in 1971 to replace the *Monthly Bulletin* which the Association had prevously published, the first editorial said:

> So much has gone wrong in the post-war period. We have under-played our strength as a large market. We have eroded confidence in our currency by inflation. We have encouraged the slacker and discouraged those who want to do a good day's work, thus under-mining individual initiative and responsibility. The young have too often been taught to despise the great contribution which our country has made to peace and stability in the world. All these mistakes and others must be rectified by a better understanding of our past and our future role in the world. Our aim is to contribute to this understanding.

The fact that the journal, now as a quarterly, has been published without interruption since 1971 seems to indicate that its message is appreciated and that it has been true to its aim.

In November 1980 the Economic Research Council sustained a severe loss in the death of Patrick de Laszlo, who had seen the Council expand its influence and prestige over the twenty years since he took over the Chairmanship from Mr John Penton. *The Times* invited me to contribute an Obituary, which was published on 7 November 1980.

PATRICK DE LASZLO
Engineering inventor and designer

Mr. Patrick de Laszlo who has died at the age of 71 will be sorely missed by those with whom he was closely associated in the business community and in economic affairs as well as his family. Son of the portrait painter, Philip de Laszlo, he was educated at Lancing and Balliol College, Oxford, where he took an Honours degree in PPE and a B.Litt in economics. Invited to stay on to teach economics he decided that he ought to learn more about practical business affairs before attempting to teach; in fact he never did return to teach.

Instead, he developed a distinguished career in industry as he found that he had a particular aptitude as an engineering inventor and designer. After lecturing in America he joined his elder brother and worked with him on the design for miniature radio valves which became universal. He then went on to become managing director of Celestion which had, some years before, invented loud speakers. This company subsequently went into the manufacture of military equipment and produced the 'proximity fuse' which later played a vital part in countering the V1 onslaught during the war.

After the war de Laszlo continued to develop new products, including fibreglass reinforced plastic hulls, pioneered by Halmatic Ltd, a company which he created for the purpose. The technique evolved by Halmatic has now been universally adopted for yachts and other small vessels. Another of his companies, McMurdo Instrument Co., developed escape lights for the Royal Navy, later adopted by many airlines. Yet another company, Digital Systems, did pioneering work in transmission of information in the form of highspeed data over low power radio systems, a technique used by UK Police Forces. He was also a director of Harwin Engineers of Portsmouth.

These activities would have been enough for most people to tackle but his enquiring mind caused him to challenge much of the orthodox thinking in the field of economics. In 1960 he became Chairman of the Economic Research Council and played a leading part in its affairs for the past 20 years. Notably, it was under his chairmanship that the Council sponsored the 'Programme for National Recovery' under whose auspices five reports were issued which contributed to a much wider understanding of the importance of money supply and the need to control Government spending.

In addition, de Laszlo played a leading role in the Association of Independent Businesses. He was chairman from 1972 until 1976 and unlike some advocates of the privately owned business sector, he well understood that it could only flourish for so long in a market economy. He spent much time and effort in developing the arguments for particular reforms such as the introduction of stock relief which the AIB proposed in July, 1974.

In 1977 he married Baroness Sharples, widow of the Governor of Bermuda who was assassinated in 1973. His first wife was Deborah, daughter of the first Viscount Greenwood by whom he had a son and four daughters. The marriage which took place in 1940 was dissolved in 1970. His second marriage to Penelope Kitson which took place in 1973 was also dissolved.

His son, Damon de Laszlo, took over the Chairmanship at the invitation of the Executive Committee and since that date has filled the post with distinction.

13

A PROGRAMME FOR NATIONAL RECOVERY

The failure of the Radcliffe Report on credit and currency to diagnose correctly the causes of inflation resulted in policies being implemented which did nothing to remedy the economic malaise which had overtaken the nation. To continue monetary policies which had been followed since the end of the war could only lead to a continuing erosion in money values and, if persisted in long enough, would lead to disaster. Realising this, I was persuaded to try and bring together a significant group of industrialists, economists and others to promote a Programme for National Recovery.

In the event, nineteen leading industrialists and economists agreed to sponsor such a programme. They were Lord Aberdare, Lord Barnby, Sir Arthur Bryant, Professor Colin Clark, Patrick de Laszlo, Sir Roy Dobson, A. Frood, Professor Denis Gabor, Edward Holloway, Graham Hutton, W. E. Luke, W. A. P. Manser, Professor C. Northcote Parkinson, Dr John Paxton, Sir Halford Reddish, Sir John Reiss, Hubert Starley, Iain M. Stewart and Antony Vickers.

The Programme stated that failure to provide an economic climate in which industry can flourish stems, on the one hand, from Government policies since the Second World War which have caused inflation to erode the value of money, and on the other, from failure to take adequate action to obviate the deep-seated suspicion which exists in many industries between employer and employee. Many others indicated their general agreement with the views we put forward in our policy statement, but for one reason or another did not want to be publicly associated with it.

Our Policy Statement was finally published in July 1967. It said:

If Britain is to recover from its present economic malaise, governments must give priority to the question of overall economic climate. The two main instruments of economic management are:
(1) Monetary Policy—varying the amount of money available as purchasing power,
(2) Fiscal Policy—varying the amount of taxation as a means of influencing the level of effective demand.

We held a well attended press conference to launch the Programme and a very satisfactory coverage was given in the national and local press. This, in turn, stimulated interest in our further research.

We were fortunate in obtaining the services of Mr Frederick Tooby to carry out the research and initial drafting of the reports, which were then edited by a group comprising Patrick de Laszlo, Chairman of the Economic Research Council; Dr John Paxton, Editor of *The Statesman's Year-Book*; Antony Vickers of Fluidrive Engineering; and myself.

The first research paper was published on 23 January 1968. It concentrated on what the authors believed to be Britain's basic weakness—inflation—which had sapped our economic strength since 1939. Once again, we had a good press, Harold Wincott in the *Financial Times* of 23 January wrote: 'The survey does a first-class and very topical job in pointing to the weaknesses in our basic policies.' Michael Blanden, writing in *The Guardian*, commented: 'This seems to be a perfectly serious effort to find out what is really wrong and to go to the root of the problems.'

Part 1 of the research paper looked at Government policies and concluded from the statistical evidence that successive administrations had failed to manage effectively the two key factors in the economy: monetary and fiscal policies. For thirty years effective demand had throughout this period outstripped the real growth rate in the economy.

Part 2 looked at present economic policies, based largely on the Paish doctrine and found that this had no validity in the post-war economy. Income from employment had not risen faster than was jointly justified by

(1)   The decreasing value of the pound; and
(2)   Increased productivity.

Wage rates had therefore *not* been the primary cause of inflation.

Part 3 found that the primary source of inflation was to be found in the way which the Exchequer deficits had been regularly financed in part by the creation of money on a scale which caused the total liquidity in the economy to expand faster than the real economic growth rate. This inflationary pressure had been added to by the ever-larger proportion of the national income taken in taxation from the private sector and then spent by governments.

Part 4 showed that balance of payments difficulties were not due to the private sector's trade with the rest of the world but to the fact that net Government expenditures overseas had persistently exceeded the surpluses earned by the private sector.

The publication of Research Paper No. 1 resulted in a considerable spate of activity in Parliament and elsewhere. On Monday 19 February 1968 on the Report stage of the National Loans Bill, Mr Robin Turton put forward amendments to the Bill which sought to implement some of the recommendations made in the Research Paper, in particular proper control by the House of Commons of Government lending both to public corporations and to local authorities.

He was supported by Sir Henry d'Avigdor-Goldsmid, who quoted from the Research Report a sentence which, he said, 'puts in clear language what I have been trying to say':

> The large haphazard flows of sterling in and out of the Exchequer, which now arise automatically out of official borrowing overseas and the working of the Exchange Equalisation Account, must be dealt with separately from the Government's borrowing and lending.

Another amendment was moved by Mr Alison, who urged the need to tighten up the whole machinery of Government financing. He said: 'The case is very formidably argued in The

National Recovery Programme. Perhaps the Chief Secretary will make an allusion to that.'

The amendments were not accepted, but there is no doubt that the views expressed in the Research Paper had begun a debate on monetary and fiscal policy, the outcome of which we are now witnessing.

When the National Loans Bill came before the House of Lords on 27 February 1968 Lord Aberdare also raised a number of points arising from the Research Paper. He said: 'I was a signatory of the document entitled "A Programme for National Recovery" which was published last July and was signed by a number of eminent economists, writers and industrialists, all far more eminent than I, and I rely very largely on their expert advice in drawing your Lordship's attention to the document. It was extremely well received and excited a great deal of interest.' He told the Lords that 'This Bill does nothing to tackle the problem of Parliamentary control, and does nothing to ensure that future Government loans represent true market borrowing.'

The publication of this first Research Report certainly stimulated debate in both Houses of Parliament and in the country as a whole this gave great encouragement to all of us who had worked so hard to produce this document and we proceeded to embark on further studies.

The Conversion of Peter Jay!

The second Research Report, entitled 'Expansion without Inflation', was published on 7 May 1968. It made it abundantly clear that Britain's economic problems were mainly in the field of public financial management, not, as was widely held at that time, in any widespread weakness of management in industry or in overspending by the private sector overseas. The report again stressed the primary source of inflation as the uncontrolled overspending by the public sector both at home and overseas.

The management of our public finances by the Executive was condemned as being 'lax and inefficient, with damaging consequences for the country's economy'. Once again, the report stimulated questions and speeches in both Houses, including an important speech in the Lords on 17 July 1968 by Lord Aberdare, a signatory to the National Recovery Programme.

Of particular interest was the intervention of the then Economic Editor of *The Times Business News*, Mr Peter Jay. In his leading article of 30 August 1968 he said:

> But the idea that nasty things like imports and inflation are particularly sensitive to demand that arises from excessive liquidity while good things like employment and profits are specially sensitive to the kind of demand that arises from liberal fiscal and credit policies belong to the thinking characteristic of Edward Holloway's 'Programme for National Recovery'. The concept of 'Expansion without Inflation' (the title of the Holloway's group second research paper) rests on the pretence that inflation is directly caused by 'the printing press', while expansion is caused by fiscal and credit stimuli, and that there is no reaction between the two phenomena. All past evidence contradicts this pious hope!

The reply we sent to *The Times* was not published, but Peter Jay returned to the fray on 19 September. Under the title 'Let's face the issue of the money supply' Mr Jay claimed that

> It is easy enough for those who have been subjected to one or more terms of economic study to refute the simple-minded quantity theory of money which appears to animate Drs Blessing, Zijlstra and Stopper. It is still easier to expose the inconsistencies in the Powell–Howell–Holloway theory that full employment and rapid expansion can be reconciled with price stability by a combination of liberal credit and fiscal policies with strict control of the money supply.

Mr Jay went on to say 'if the British authorities are not to make a free present of a cheap political platform to the likes of Messrs Powell, Howell and Holloway, they should initiate in their regular commentaries a fuller treatment than at present of money supply trends and of their effects'. Although Mr Jay claimed that he had received telephone advice from Paris that there had been a significant fall in money supply in the last quarter, he discovered only a few days later that money supply had been rising at an annual rate of 9.9 per cent during the second quarter. On this subject he had to change his mind, and in due course admitted that the behaviour of the money supply in Britain was increasingly regarded as a serious blot on the Government's management of the economy.

Overseas Trade and Payments

We then turned our attention to the question of the balance of payments and invisible earnings and Report No.3 under this title was published on 24 January 1969. Once again there was a wide coverage in the press Harold Wincott devoted a favourable full-length article on the subject in the *Financial Times* on 8 February and the Lombard Column, then written by Gordon Tether, also in the *FT*, commented: 'The National Recovery Programme's economists have hit a considerable number of nails on the head in setting out the background to Britain's persistent economic malaise.'

The report said that our balance of payments troubles in recent years had been caused by Government spending overseas which had persistently outpaced the growing cash inflow from the private sector's trading and investment overseas. This theme was subsequently referred to in questions and debates in the House of Commons.

The claim that taxation not only should, but could be substantially reduced was made in Report No.4, which was entitled 'Taxation: The Financing of Public Expenditure', published at the end of 1969.

Our final report was published in May 1970 and it posed the question 'Is Britain squandering its resources?' It postulated that if the country used its resources more fully a much higher growth rate could be obtained. It estimated that an annual growth rate of 6½ per cent would be 'a modest target' when the full extent of the under-use of resources is taken into account.

The report pointed out that 'more successful nations acknowledge the advantage of the market economy and the private enterprise system, but in Britain enterprise is subject to more substantial political attack than in any other major industrial nation of the Western world. As a result British managers tend to be on the defensive and are discouraged from vigorously pursuing the most advanced techniques which have proved successful elsewhere.'

For this report we sought the assistance of Mr Frank Broadway, who played an essential role in the formulation of the Paper. It also owes much to the thinking of the late Antony Vickers, whose writings have stressed the need for a reappraisal of our basic economic assumptions. In his book *Expansion or Explosion*, published in 1955, he wrote as an engineer, very conscious of the failure to use the advantages given by the immense strides in science and technology which, if used, could lead mankind to increased freedom, prosperity and peace for all peoples.

It is pleasant to record that much of the thinking, particularly in the monetary field, which we put forward in this series has now become very much part of current economic policy. When we first put these ideas forward they met with a considerable amount of scepticism on the part of the establishment, but they are now an accepted part of thinking in our political life.

The outcome of all these efforts brought about the establishment of a special research fund to facilitate further research, and several publications have resulted, notably *Excessive Taxes Lead to 'Stag-flation'* and *Excessive Taxes Lead to Inflation and Unemployment*. We owe a debt to Sir David Barran and other industrialists for providing us with the necessary funds to enable us to undertake the considerable volume of research needed to make these publications possible.

14

DIALOGUE WITH DOWNING STREET

In the early part of 1968 we attempted to persuade Harold Wilson, the Prime Minister, of the validity of the case we had made in the studies carried out under the auspices of the National Recovery Programme. This had demonstrated that the private sector of the economy had consistently lived well within its income and largely saved, while the public sector had persistently overspent its income. As a result, in the economy as a whole, total expenditure had exceeded total income, forcing the country into debt overseas.

We were concerned that the Government appeared to have ignored our case and remained convinced that it was the private sector of the economy which had been the cause of our troubles by persistently living beyond its means. In the light of this, we decided to enlist the support of a number of leading economists* to persuade the Prime Minister, Harold Wilson, to consider postponing three Bills then before Parliament.

The Bills in question were the Transport Bill, the Transport Holding Bill and the Industrial Expansion Bill. Taken together, they involved an expenditure of several millions a year from public funds. In the letter sent to the Prime Minister by the nine signatories it said that confidence abroad was likely to be undermined by 'this massive expenditure', and it was urged that, for the good of the nation, this legislation should be postponed.

Mr Wilson replied to this letter on 10 April 1968. In his reply he explained at some length the reason behind each of the Bills

---

* Dr Paul Einzig; Edward Holloway; Graham Hutton; Patrick de Laszlo; Dr John Paxton; J. W. Nisbet; C. Northcote Parkinson; G. S. A. Wheatcroft; and Jack Wiseman.

referred to in our letter. He maintained that these were necessary in pursuit of the modernisation and restructuring of the British economy. His letter concluded:

Each of the measures referred to in your letter is concerned basically with the need to secure more economic use of national resources. Far from being postponable, each of them in its own way is a necessary contribution to the overall objective of strengthening and modernising our economy.

This reply gave us little satisfaction, and we decided to make our case in rather more detail. The following letter was delivered to the Prime Minister on 9 March:

Dear Prime Minister,
    Thank you for your letter of 10th April. We greatly appreciate the fact that you took the trouble to write to us personally.
    We would also like to express our appreciation of the conspicuous improvement, continued under your Government, in the publication of statistics of the national economy by the Central Statistical Office and the Bank of England. However, analysis of these statistics has led us to the conclusion that the balance of payments crises, which have imposed such a strain on the country and ultimately to devaluation, were not basically due to gross excess of visible imports over exports, but to lack of confidence in the reliability of the value of sterling as a reserve currency which caused foreign depositors to withdraw their funds from English banks. Furthermore, this lack of confidence arose from the fact that foreign depositors were aware from published statistics that the value of the domestic Pound was being steadily diminished by inflation.
    In our view, the cause of inflation is that deficitory expenditure by the public sector has not been covered and financed entirely by borrowing from the non-bank private sector, but rather from the Central Bank which automatically enlarged the basis of all bank credit year by year. This money has ended up in the hands of the private sector and re-appeared as additional deposits with the banks.

The proof of this is that net deposits by UK residents with the banks expanded from £9,238 million at the end of September, 1964, to £11,310 million at the end of September, 1967. This was an increase of 22.5% over the three years, representing an average yearly rate of expansion of liquidity of 7%, whereas over the same period the real economic growth averaged only 1.9% per annum.

Point 10 of the Letter of Intent to the Managing Director of I.M.F. on 23rd November, 1967, makes it clear that the factor to be kept under joint review by your Government and the Managing Director of the I.M.F, is the effectiveness of fiscal policy in holding down the Exchequer's borrowing requirement with the clear implication that it is this restraint which will 'play the most important role in making room for the needed improvement in the balance of payments.'

Whilst we respect the desire of your Government to modernise and restructure the economy, we cannot avoid grave misgivings about the proposed methods set out in your letter of 10th April which imply substantial further 'borrowing' from the banking system. It can only result in further inflation which will have to be counteracted by even more rigid control of prices and wages. This, we believe, will stifle initiative, breed growing resentment, and end by precipitating industrial unrest.

For this reason we ask you again to postpone the Industrial Expansion Bill (which, of course, does not prevent individual schemes being submitted to Parliament) and to delete the clauses in the Transport Bill which involve additional calls on Public funds.

Yours faithfully
Edward Holloway
Graham Hutton
Patrick de Laszlo
J. W. Nisbet
John Paxton
C. Northcote Parkinson
G. S. A. Wheatcroft

On 10th June the Prime Minister again replied to us and showed quite clearly that the case we had put forward had not been accepted. He wrote:

10 Downing Street,
Whitehall,
LONDON, S.W.1.

June 10, 1968

Dear Mr Holloway,

Thank you for your further letter of May 9.

I do not accept that a case has been made out for saying that the cause of this country's balance of payments problem has originated in the volume and method of financing of Government expenditure since 1964. Nor can the balance of payments deficits be explained simply in terms of confidence factors.

As official international comparisons by the Organisation for Economic Co-operation and Development shows, ours is neither the most highly taxed country, nor does Government expenditure absorb more of our resources than in many other countries in comparable circumstances. The Government has given proof of its determination to restrain the growth in public expenditure and, as the Chancellor made clear in his Budget statement, the borrowing requirement is to be drastically reduced.

Nor do I believe that we can hope to put an end to balance of payments deficits merely by operating on the rate of increase in the money supply. Our balance of payments deficits go back well beyond 1964 and are not to be explained in terms of the increase in the money supply since that date. The effective remedy must lie in a large shift in the allocation of resources so as to permit an improvement in the balance of payments and the Government has already taken the necessary fiscal measures to enable the balance of payments targets to be achieved.

The Industrial Expansion Act is intended to help industry to increase productivity so that we can increase our share in world exports of manufactures and reduce imports through substitution of home products. Projects likely to be brought forward under the enabling powers in the Act—and I take it that it is to these that you are referring rather than to the specific provisions for ship-building, Cunard and particular aircraft projects—will have been carefully screened so that assistance is given only for schemes likely to strengthen our industrial performance. Government assistance will be given only if funds cannot be made available from private sources and their provision in such cases would not involve a larger use of resources than if they were provided privately. You admit that the absence of these enabling powers would not prevent individual schemes being submitted to Parliament. Thus the sole point at issue is which of these two possible procedures would provide the most effective form of control and of Parliamentary scrutiny.

Now that the Bill has become law, we propose to seek the approval of the House of Commons under the new powers for the Ministry of Technology's contribution to the merger of computer manufacturers. I do not want to deal here with the merits of this particular scheme but, so far as concerns the presentation of the scheme to Parliament, the detailed explanation submitted in seeking approval for the Order may be found to compare well with that in many past pieces of legislation. Governments of different political complexions have provided public money for industry over many years, and the need for an Act of Parliament cannot be said always to have resulted in good choices and sensible economic decisions. Nobody can guarantee that the new procedure will have this effect either. But it is certainly one of our objectives to improve the economic appraisal and administrative handling of such cases in the future.

The financial consequences of the Transport Bill have been greatly exaggerated. For example, the effect of writing-off part of the capital debt of the Railways and Waterways Board under the Bill is notional since the interest on this debt has never been found by the Boards from their own resources. The money had already been lost before the present Government came to power.

As regards new expenditure, it is envisaged that specific grants under the Bill will amount to a little over £100 million a year, of which the grants for the loss-making passenger services of British Rail will account for about half. On the other hand, the Bill will bring to an end the present open-ended systems of revenue deficit grants to the Boards, under which the Government paid British Rail alone over £150 million last year (including £30 million interest which is now to be written-off). The new system of specific grants which the Government propose will permit a much better comparison of costs and benefits, so ensuring better value for money and the elimination of wasteful expenditure.

So far as the other assistance to public transport is concerned, one of the main aims is to encourage the development of facilities which will lessen the need for much heavier expenditure on roads.

Yours sincerely

(Sgd.) HAROLD WILSON

The correspondence, which had been quite widely reported in the national press, had also aroused some interest among Members of Parliament. As a result, a question had been put to the Prime Minister by Mr John Hunt, the Conservative Member for Bromley. He asked Mr Wilson 'What reply he has sent to the letter he received on May 9th from seven economists, headed by Mr Edward Holloway, on the causes of the current inflationary pressures within the economy.'

There was an amusing background to the posing of this question. We had received no reply to our letter of 9 May until lunchtime on the day the question was due for a reply. In fact, the reply was delivered to me by hand only an hour or two before Question Time in the House, so that the Prime Minister was able to reply 'that he had arranged for his correspondence with this group of political economists to be placed in the Library'.

In a supplementary Mr Hunt commented:

> These distinguished economists drew attention to a worldwide lack of confidence in Britain arising from continuing failure to contain inflation.
> Does the Prime Minister not feel that the latest depressing figures of industrial production, coupled with the ever-increasing trend of Government expenditure, is compelling evidence of the validity of the case which these economists have made?
> (*Opposition cheers*)
> *Mr Wilson:* I think these distinguished political economists succeeded in putting into economic jargon some of the more ignorant shibboleths of Opposition members.
> (*Ministerial cheers*)

Mr Robin Turton, the Conservative Member for Thirsk and Malton, finally succeeded in getting a categorical statement from the Prime Minister regarding his views on the subject. He asked: 'Would the Prime Minister make clear whether he agrees or disagrees with the verdict of these economists that the prime cause of inflation has been the fact that in the past three years expenditure which amounts to over £3000m has not been financed or covered by borrowing from the private non-banking sector but from the central banks?' Mr Wilson replied: 'The answer is no. I do not agree with their analysis or conclusions.'

Although this gave little encouragement, we decided we would have one more go at the Prime Minister and we wrote to him again on 9 July. While we thanked him for giving us 'such a full statement of his views we pointed out that his reply had done nothing to explain how and why net bank deposits by UK residents expanded by 22.5 per cent. Our letter went on to say:

In the course of an exchange during Question Time in the House of Commons on 20th June you said that you did not agree with our analysis or our conclusions. Yet a supplementary table in *Financial Statistics* for April 1968 confirms that liquid funds in the possession of the personal sector increased from £15,464 million at the end of 1962 to £22,034 million at the end of 1967, or by 43 per cent over the five years. So there is undeniable evidence that there was an average of £400 of potential spending-money in the hands of every man, woman and child in the entire population at the end of 1967, and that this average holding per capita had increased from £292 during the period.

Our research has been based on the new accounts of Sector Financing and Flows of Funds, which were introduced in September 1963, published in the Bank of England *Quarterly Bulletin* of December 1967. The importance of these accounts in providing a fuller understanding of the functioning of the economy has not in our view been properly appreciated. Since you disagree with our analysis and conclusions as to the way in which this additional liquidity has come into circulation, surely it is of paramount importance that an official explanation should be made available. Will you not arrange for this to be done?

The final reply dated 5 August came from 10 Downing Street but unlike the previous correspondence, it was not signed by the Prime Minister. However, it did show some common ground, and it gave an indication that the Government's views had moved a little way towards the thinking which had inspired our letters. The letter said:

Dear Mr Holloway,

The Prime Minister has asked me to thank you for your further letter of July 9th.

The Government share at least some common ground with you in that it attaches considerable importance to the size of its borrowing requirement and to the liquidity of the economy.

And later:

Appropriate monetary policy is one element in the whole range of policies which the Government is using in order to strengthen our international position, and this aspect cannot be considered in isolation so we felt that we could rest our case in the hope that further enlightenment would follow.

Despite the fact that the Prime Minister had declared so emphatically that he agreed with neither the analysis nor the conclusions expressed in our correspondence, there was clearly some shift in opinion inside the Government towards the realisation that Government borrowing in the banking sector had a direct inflationary effect.

Having corresponded with Mr Wilson with some effect, the question of writing again to 10 Downing Street arose some five years later. By October 1973, Mr Edward Heath had taken over as Prime Minister and his Government appeared to be going back on policies on which they had been elected. Now referred to as the famous 'U-turn', the Government was on the point of publishing its proposals for Stage Three of its pay and prices policy. In these circumstances we thought it well to obtain the support of a number of leading economists to warn the Prime Minister of the dangers of continuing policies which would inevitably lead to increased inflation. Thus, we got ten economists, including Professor G. C. Allen, Professor S. H. Frankel, Professor Harry Johnson and Mr Graham Hutton to join us in making the point that 'inflation is essentially a monetary malady which can only be put right by monetary discipline'. Our letter said:

We believe that inflation arises primarily from the excessive expansion of the money supply which, as far as the U.K. is concerned, is shown by the figures published by the Bank of England.

We went on to trace the source of the rapid rise in the money supply to the growth in Government spending and the overall size of the Government's spending deficit which is having to be financed by borrowing from the banks. It is never easy to reduce Government spending, yet, if inflation is to be contained it must be done and the sooner the better. We went on to say:

> We realise that it will be difficult for you, that it will cause disappointment and may even result in some hardship, yet these are temporary effects which will be more than counter-balanced by the long-term gains, both internal and international, from stabilising the value of our money.

As previously we sent out a press release covering the despatch of the letter to Mr Heath with the usual embargo. Unfortunately, *The Guardian* jumped the gun by reporting on the day before the official date and thus prevented us from getting the widespread coverage which we know would have been given in the nationals and other media. Nothing is so dead with the press than a story which has already been published in some other paper! I took up the matter with the Editor of *The Guardian*, who apologised, but this did nothing to remedy the situation.

Thus our initiative got off to a bad start, and history shows that the Government's failure to take note of the serious consequences of their actions led to a rip-roaring inflation from which we have not yet recovered.

15

LECTURE PROGRAMME

Among many activities which have engaged my attention since the early 1930s has been the lecture programme, which entailed travelling all over the country to speak at Rotary Club lunches and Round Table groups, as well as various womens' organisations. I joined the speakers' panel of the Commonwealth Industries Association after the war, under whose auspices I talked about the sterling area, international trade and payments and similar topics. Later, I also joined the panel of the Chartered Institute of Secretaries.

The lectures I enjoyed most, however, were those I carried out in the 1950s and 1960s at public and grammar schools to fifth- and sixth-form boys and girls. I was encouraged to undertake this activity by an old and valued friend, Dr John Paxton, who was, at the time, teaching economics at Millfield school in Somerset. He had first come to my attention some months after the 1945 election, when he wrote to me from some remote part of the world, hoping that I had been successful in my election campaign! John pointed out to me that few schools had encouraged the study of economics as a specific subject, and so far as it was dealt with at all, it was a by-product of history and geography.

Accordingly, I circulated letters to headmasters and a number of leading public and grammar schools offering to lecture to fifth- and sixth-formers on a selected list of economic topics which I thought would be of interest.

The response to this circular letter was most encouraging and, as a result, I was able to build up a significant programme of school lectures which covered a period of over twenty years. During this period I went to most of the leading public schools, for both boys and girls, and in some cases, I had a regular arrangement to lecture once or twice a year. It was a most worthwhile exercise, and the questions which followed the lectures showed a very keen interest and a desire to know and understand more about the economy and the way it operated.

Perhaps the most successful, from my point of view, were the lectures at Bradfield College in Berkshire. The headmaster at that time was Anthony Chenevix-Trench, who later went to Eton. The rule he made for lectures at Bradfield was that the boys decided on the topics and the lectures themselves, without any interference from any of the staff, none of whom attended the lectures. Thus it was with particular pleasure that I gave a series of talks covering three or four weekly visits, and was able to develop a theme more fully than was possible in a single visit.

Needless to say, Millfield was on my list, and I well remember the occasion when Dr Paxton announced at the conclusion of the lecture that I had some copies of my new book *Money the Decisive Factor*, available and would autograph any copies purchased. The entire class formed a queue round the lecture room and I had what seemed to me to be 'the sale of the century'!

One rather less happy occasion was when I arrived at a school on a Sunday evening to find the headmaster entertaining a number of special guests to a dinner party, who certainly did not expect me to arrive in the middle of it. I had travelled, as instructed, to an hotel where, it was stated on the invitation, a taxi would pick me up and take me to the school. I waited vainly for the taxi to turn up and, as it did not arrive, I took a taxi to the school, to be given a very frosty reception.

Apparently my booking to lecture had been confirmed just before the summer holidays, and the secretary had failed to note this in the diary. Subsequently, an admiral had been booked to lecture at the same time on Monday as had been arranged for me. When this was explained, the atmosphere grew less frosty, but it was not a very enjoyable experience. Considering the many engagements I undertook during this period, it was one of the very few which went wrong. Among other audiences, I spoke to societies at Oxford and Cambridge as well as Birmingham University, but these were a lot less spontaneous to talk to.

It is difficult to judge the value of these lectures on subjects which covered much of my thinking on monetary problems, but, remembering the influence on my own approach to economic and related matters which arose from reading Eimar O'Duffy's book back in the 1930s, I had hopes that they were not entirely without useful results.

I was very impressed on one occasion at St Swithun's, a girls' school at Winchester, where I went fairly regularly. Here again, the policy was to give the girls the responsibility of entertaining the lecturer to tea before the talk, and very well they did this. After one lecture I was walking to my car with a number of girls still asking questions. One of them said, 'Last year you told us so and so, and this year you said something different'. I had to explain this apparent contradiction, but what impressed me was the fact that my lecture given a year ago was actually remembered twelve months later!

The talks I gave over this period were, of course, not only school lectures. I spoke at various conferences and seminars organised by industrial groups and I particularly remember one in the Birmingham area in 1955. The series, covering various aspects of the economy both internal and international, was to be given to a group of young apprentices. Some twenty of them attended the lectures given in the firm's time, and when I saw them sitting waiting for the first talk my heart sank into my boots. There they sat, utterly bored, or so they appeared, and with hardly a flicker of interest showing by any of them. Used, as I was, to the keenness shown by sixth formers, I felt that this was attempting the impossible.

However, I gave five talks to this listless and unappreciative (so I thought) group of young men. The sixth and final session, I told them, was to be a questions session, when I would answer written questions to be handed in during the previous week. To my amazement, when I went to give the final talk I was presented with a list of questions which showed that, in spite of their apparent indifference, they had really understood what it was I was trying to tell them. So much for appearances.

On another occasion I was asked to talk on international trade to a weekend conference of dock-workers, organised by the London Dock Labour Board. This was a particularly lively audience, but one that I found had a completely misconceived idea of the contribution which Britain had made in the sphere of world trade and particularly in the Commonwealth. They had firmly got it into their minds that our role had been one of exploitation, with no redeeming features. Nothing I could say would alter this firmly held view.

Fortunately, however, I was followed by a young Indian from the High Commission, who proceeded to confirm all I had tried to say about the contribution made by Britain to the Indian sub-continent. While accepting that it had not all been good, the balance was, in his opinion, in our favour. While the dockers would not take it from me, they were much impressed when told by one of the 'oppressed people' that Britain's role had, on balance, been beneficial.

One result of this lecture was that it was proposed that I should give regular talks at these conferences but, as so often happened in my experience, this idea was banned by the Establishment without any real explanation.

I suppose everyone who lectures has his favourite story, but the one I liked the best was told me by a member of the Economic Reform Club, the Rev. W. G. Peck. As a young parson working for the Industrial Christian Fellowship, he started his lecturing programme with an invitation to talk to a small group of working-men. On his arrival at the station, he was met and told that it was half an hour's walk to the place where the talk was to be given. On arrival, he was invited to partake of a meal which consisted of cold rice pudding.

This experience prompted him to take precautions against similar problems. So when he set out for his second engagement, he was determined not to be caught out again. So he laid on ample supplies of meat pies, sandwiches, cake and fruit. However, on this occasion he was met by a chauffeur complete with Rolls, and was taken to a large mansion where he was given a splendid dinner. The butler had insisted on taking his bag on arrival, and to his horror, when he was shown to his room, all his clothes were neatly laid out and on the shelf there were his pies, sandwiches, cake and fruit beautifully arranged.

Now that I am no longer able to travel all over the country giving lectures, I still treasure the many comments sent in following my visits to a number of schools. Examples of the very encouraging reception I received are the following:

Royal Masonic School 24/10/59
Mr Holloway impressed the boys as being a master of his subject. He was clear, simple and interesting. The large number of intelligent questions at the end from his audience made it clear that he had started their minds working, and the comments made to myself afterwards confirmed this impression. I can say unreservedly that it was a great success.

Ardingly College 16/10/59
First class. I consider him to be a highly gifted exponent of economic matters.

King William College, Isle of Man 3/10/59
A very good lecture indeed in which very abstruse problems were put to an audience of 15–18½ very clearly. There were a lot of good questions by boys from a variety of Sixth form 'sides'.

Chesterfield Saint Helena School 9/10/59
The girls, the majority of whom are in the Sixth form, found the lecture most interesting and stimulating, as indeed they have found Mr Holloway's previous talks at the school.

Barnstaple Grammar School 13/10/59
Mr. Holloway lectured on 'Britain's Changing Economy' with great clarity and command of his subject. Though it was not a topic of obvious attraction to schoolboys, the sensible questions asked at the end showed that he had succeeded in putting it across. He answered these questions fully and interestingly.

Tiverton Grammar School 15/10/59
An exceptionally clear survey of a wide field. Challenging and stimulating, it has evoked considerable discussion since among the Sixth forms. We hope to hear Mr Holloway again.

Queen Mary School, Lytham 5/11/59
Mr Holloway made a valuable contribution to the knowledge of the Sixth forms on Thursday. His lecture 'How Britain Earns her Living' was a clear and interesting talk, which stimulated the girls, gave them much factual information, and a vivid interpretation of

it, and has led to many questions. It is especially helpful that a lecture on subjects depending on a wide background of knowledge should make the girls eager to read more. We hope that Mr Holloway will be able to come again.

Nelson Thomlinson School, Wigton 20/11/59
Lucid, attractive delivery; facts carefully prepared and marshalled. Audience interested and impressed. This is the second time we have had Mr Holloway and we are looking forward to a third visit in due course.

Carlisle Grammar School 19/11/59
Very stimulating and interesting. The boys were impressed by Mr Holloway's command of the subject ('The Sterling Area') and the force and clarity of his answers to questions. . . All agreed that the talk was well worth while and it will lead, I believe, to reading on the subject.

These are just a few of the comments sent in from head teachers after the lectures. In one period of twelve months I covered 30,000 miles by car in addition to many journeys by train. It was exhausting but well worth while. With great regret I had to discontinue a full programme of lectures in 1970, since when I have had to cut down my engagements considerably.

16

UNITED EUROPE

Opinion as to the advisability of Britain joining the European Economic Community was very divided within the membership of the Economic Research Council, as indeed it was throughout the country. As an organisation, the ERC was not able, therefore, to play a part in the acute controversy which raged from 1961, when Harold Macmillan as Prime Minister announced the Government's intention to apply for membership. Individual members of the Council were, of course, completely free to take their own line on this controversial issue, and the more I studied the question the more hostile I became to the idea of our joining the EEC under the terms of the Treaty of Rome.

This was a change of view, for originally I had been favourably disposed to the general idea of European unity, always provided that in joining in a European association we did no harm to our Commonwealth and sterling-area ties. For a time I was associated with the United Europe Movement and spoke on their behalf. This was mainly as a result of the persuasion of Lady (Juliet) Rhys Williams, a supporter of the Economic Reform Club, who was also for a time Honorary Secretary of the Economic Research Council.

My views on the need for European unity had been influenced by various personal experiences which had made me realise how important it was to bring the nations of Europe into closer harmony in the economic and cultural aspects of their lives. The first shock I received was very soon after the end of the First World War. I wanted to go to France for a holiday and it was therefore necessary to apply for a passport. The only passport I had previously travelled on was a rather splendid parchment document issued by the Consul in Odessa when my mother returned to England with my sister and I after the death of my father.

When I applied for a passport in London, the fun started. It was at the time of the Arcos raids, when the mere mention of Russia caused every suspicion to be aroused. At the passport office I duly presented my birth certificate showing my date of birth as 13 and 26 July (Russian and English dates), and that I was born in Rovno in the state of Volhynia. This was enough to arouse the deepest suspicions, and I was immediately sent to a special room to be interviewed. Was my father British? Was he born in England? Was my mother British? Where was she born.

I had not anticipated all this and could not give all the details requested, and it was then explained to me that if my father had also been born abroad, then I had no right to British citizenship. This was a terrible shock: I was young and rather inexperienced in such matters. As a special concession I was, after several other interviews, granted a passport for a period of six months for France only.

The matter was finally cleared up when, as a result of some investigation, I was able to obtain a copy of my father's birth certificate from Somerset House, showing that he had been born in Derby. But the threat that had he been born overseas, I would not be able to claim British citizenship was very salutory.

Shortly after this I went on a visit to Germany and Austria. With some other young people I was invited to a Hungarian monastery in Vienna for an evening get-together with other students. On arrival we found that we were in very mixed company. As well as our Hungarian hosts there were Austrians, Poles, Czechs and Germans as well as we British. The atmosphere was one of great goodwill, and some splendid refreshments were served and greatly enjoyed, whereupon our Hungarian hosts produced maps showing how the Eastern European Territories had been partitioned as a result of the Treaty of the Trianon, which had followed the more famous Treaty of Versailles.

Within minutes of the production of these maps the atmosphere changed completely. Our hitherto friendly and pleasant gathering dissolved into fierce arguments between Poles, Czechs, Austrians, Germans, etc., and before long actual physical fighting broke out. We British, who were completely ignorant of the issues involved, were appalled and did our best to calm the antagonists. We had our first lesson in international politics, and this made me realise that the seeds of the Second World War had already been sown.

The fact that the Treaty of Trianon imposed in 1920 is still having a baleful influence 64 years afterwards on middle-European affairs was clearly demonstrated by a report published in *The Times* on 19 November 1984. Richard Bassett, who had visited Transylvania, wrote: 'Of all the displaced minorities caused by the readjustment of Central Europe's frontiers after the First World War, none arouses more passions than the fate of Transylvania's two million Hungarians.'

Another pre-war memory is of the period just before the Second World War broke out. I was very keen to see how things were in France and Italy, and decided to take a brief holiday, travelling through France, where some war-time precautions were already in evidence. I finally reached San Remo in the north of Italy and stayed for a couple of weeks at an hotel where I was the only British resident. The hotel was full of German workers who were given a free holiday by the German Government, but fortunately they were given separate accommodation for meals. We could hear them chanting their 'Heil Hitlers' and the 'Horst Wessel' song, which in no way added to the enjoyment of the other hotel guests.

The strange thing was that as the only Britisher in the hotel I was given much attention by both Germans and Italians, who, on finding themselves alone with me, proceeded to condemn their allies in no uncertain terms. The Germans disliked and despised the Italians, while the Italians were not slow to express their feelings about the Germans who were invading their country in such numbers. The only thing they seemed to agree about was their desire to be friends with the British, a message which they implored me to take back home with me.

I became friendly with one German who was staying at the hotel as an individual guest, and he and I discussed the worsening international situation at great length. He was bitterly opposed to the Hitler regime and all it stood for.

One evening we were talking about the number of Germans

who listened to the British radio, and he made a remark that amazed me. He said 'millions of Germans prayed every night that Britain would declare war on Germany as this was the only way they could see to get rid of Hitler'. When I said that I could not imagine saying such a thing about my own country, he said that until one actually experienced living under a totalitarian dictatorship such as Hitler and the Nazis had imposed upon his country, one could not begin to appreciate the true horror of the situation.

I travelled back to England in a very sober and thoughtful mood, feeling that I was truly living in a madhouse. So-called allies hating each other, both wanting to be friends with Britain, but at the same time a war between us was becoming increasingly inevitable!

These and other experiences over the pre-war period had made me realise the need for creating a greater spirit of unity among the nations of Europe, who were, once again, contemplating the extreme folly of fighting each other and destroying their people's lives and wealth. When the idea of a United Europe movement was launched after the war I found myself in favour.

There was, however, one proviso, so far as I was concerned. Britain had, over the centuries, built up a valuable association with other nations outside Europe, principally with the nations of the former British Empire, which had translated itself into the Commonwealth. The ties in trade and the payments system of the sterling area were, to my mind, very important to us. So when I realised that to join the European Community under the terms of the Treaty of Rome would mean a surrender of sovereignty in some areas, and that our close and valuable association in trade and in the sterling area in the Commonwealth would be gravely weakened, I became more and more convinced that if Britain became embroiled in the economic and agricultural technicalities associated with the Common Market it would be a grave error of judgement.

My own preference was to expand the European Free Trade Association into an Atlantic Free Trade Area, to include the USA and Canada. There was some influential support for this concept on both sides of the Atlantic, Senator Javits of New York told the Pilgrims in London that Britain should 'leapfrog' the Common Market and join the USA, Canada and Australia in an Atlantic Free Trade Area. In my view had this idea been adopted it could have revolutionised the world monetary system by deepening the creative interdependence of dollar and sterling, both of which played an important role in the international payments system, about which there is now so much concern.

But this was not to be. The Rome Treaty, setting up the Common Market and Euratom, had been signed in March 1957 and came into force on 1 January 1958. In 1961, the UK requested negotiations aimed at membership of the Common Market, along with Denmark. President de Gaulle of France resisted our approach and it was not until October 1971 that the House of Commons approved entry by 356 votes against 244: a majority of 112.

Thus the long and bitter debate which divided public opinion and political parties was over. There is no doubt that the campaign had been heavily weighted on the side of the pro-marketeers, who were guilty of some very dubious argument in favour of joining the EEC which have since become apparent. Some leaflets issued by the European Movement stated 'You've lost £7 a week in your pay packet', 'More and cheaper housing inside the Common Market' and similar slogans which were, to say the least, somewhat misleading. Many of them have been shown to be false in the light of experience, leading to a growing sense of disillusionment by the people of Britain. Opinion polls have now shown a majority against membership.

Typical of the lengths to which the pro-market element would go to conceal the facts from the British people was an incident in which I was personally involved.

Sir Henry Kelliher, a prominent industrialist in New Zealand with whom I had corresponded on monetary questions for many years, drew my attention to a resolution which had been passed by the New Zealand Returned Services Association and supported by the Returned Services League of Australia. As a result, he arranged for Mr R.B. Reed, President of the New Zealand Association, to send me the following cable:

At recent annual meeting the Dominion Council of the Returned Services Association of New Zealand the following resolution was carried unanimously. (Quote) That this Dominion Council being under an obligation to loyally uphold and defend the Constitution of New Zealand as member of the British Commonwealth of Nations and being of opinion that the fabric of the British Commonwealth will be undermined by the entry of the United Kingdom into the European Economic Community because the sovereignty of Her Majesty The Queen would be substantially surrendered and recalling the sacrifices of New Zealanders in two World Wars in defence of the British way of life resolves that the deep concern felt by all New Zealand Returned Servicemen be drawn to the attention of the British Commonwealth Ex-Services League and further resolves that the Dominion Executive Committee be requested to take any action necessary to defend and maintain the links which bind the British Commonwealth of Nations together under the Sovereignty of Her Majesty The Queen (unquote). This resolution was transmitted to the British Legion requesting release to Her Majesty the news media and other influential persons but this important and patriotic message was withheld by the Legion Council on grounds the Legion is non-political.

The Auckland RSA having obtained opinion from leading Queen's Counsel is shocked to learn that sovereignty of Her Majesty will be seriously imperilled and the Royal Prerogative affecting the issue of money abrogated if Britain enters the EEC on terms set out in Treaty of Rome and the Special Arrangement. My Association expressed its deep concern by reinforcing the above resolution in a lengthy cable to British Legion of Servicemen through Dr Bremner our London representative but this message was inexplicably suppressed. *We have just received confirmation of Conference resolution passed by the Returned Services League of Australia representing 263,000 Returned Servicemen who strongly support the views expressed in our cables.* Request you take urgent action as indicated and ask Sir Arthur Bryant to incorporate in his petition.

R. B. REED
PRESIDENT AUCKLAND RSA

(Unfortunately the words in italics were omitted from the cable as received due to an operator's error in London.)
On receipt of this cable I sent copies to all Members of

Parliament and a number of Peers with the following covering memorandum:

NEW ZEALAND RETURNED SERVICES ASSOCIATION

I have just received an important cable from New Zealand which sets out the views of the Dominion Council of the Returned Services Association of New Zealand on the question of Britain and the Common Market. The membership of the Association is one hundred thousand strong and it seems to me essential that their views, coming from men who have fought to defend the British way of life, should be made known to every Member of Parliament before the coming debates on this vital question.

A disturbing feature is that a previous cable, sent to the New Zealand representative of the British Commonwealth Ex-Services League, has apparently been suppressed.

In view of the large number of New Zealanders who are anxious that their views should be made known to the British Parliament and electorate, I hope you will give the contents of the cable your careful attention.

At the same time, I sent the text of the cable to the press with a covering press release:

BRITAIN AND THE COMMON MARKET

Deep Concern expressed by
New Zealand Returned Servicemen

A copy of a cable received by Edward Holloway from the Dominion Council of the Returned Services Association of New Zealand has today been circulated to every Member of Parliament and to certain Peers. The cable (copy enclosed) giving the text of a resolution carried unanimously at the Association's Annual Meeting, expresses deep concern arising from the proposal that the United Kingdom should join the European Economic Community, and states as their opinion that this action will undermine the fabric of the British Commonwealth because 'The sovereignty of Her Majesty The Queen would be substantially surrendered'. The membership of the RSA is one hundred thousand strong.

In a covering letter sent to MPs with the copy of the cable, Mr Edward Holloway says: 'It seems essential that these views, coming from men who have fought to defend the British way of life, should be made known to every MP before the coming debates on this vital question.'

A disturbing feature is that a previous cable sent to the New Zealand representative of the British Commonwealth Ex-Services League was 'inexplicably suppressed'.

Not one word about this important statement of views sent on behalf of a large number of New Zealand Servicemen, and supported by the Australian Returned Services League, found its way into the UK press, although it was mentioned in New Zealand. Apparently the views of men who fought with us in the last war were not considered of sufficient interest to be given space in our news media.

The question of suppression of the cable was taken up by Sir Robin Turton in a speech in the Common Market Debate on 21 October. Following this, the matter was discussed in the House of Commons. But the people of Britain were kept in ignorance of the views of the New Zealand and Australian ex-servicemen, which I still believe to be a scandal.

17

LETTERS TO THE PRESS

There is no doubt that one of the important methods of getting ideas across to the public at large is by means of letters to the press. Throughout the whole period covered in this book it has been of great value when one of the nationals has given space to a letter setting out some aspect of economic policy in line with our general theme of reform of the monetary system.

Generally speaking, the press have been co-operative, particularly in recent years, though this was not always so. I recall that in the period when Geoffrey Dawson edited *The Times* we seldom managed to get any response. When Sir Reginald Rowe and I sent a joint letter, we had a reply from *The Times* signed by Barrington-Ward, in which he indicated that our letter could not be published, but he thought that we would find a more sympathetic view would be taken in a few months' time. Sure enough, when he became editor shortly afterwards, and during the period of his editorship, we found a much greater readiness to publish our letters.

Looking back over the past twenty years, a very considerable number of letters have been published in *The Times*, *Daily Telegraph* and *The Financial Times* and for the record it may be of interest to include a selection of these.

Financial Times Friday, 28 April 1961
Economic Regulator
The Chancellor of the Exchequer is to be congratulated in giving recognition to the need for a more adequate regulator to control the economy. Many of us have been urging the necessity for this for a long time and it is undoubtedly a step in the right direction that a somewhat belated attempt is being made to introduce more adequate machinery.

Unfortunately, he appears to have started at the wrong end. By

148

proposing to regulate spending by increases in purchase-tax and the very controversial pay-roll tax, he intends to reduce the ability to spend, but in doing so, he will force prices in an upward direction.

If we accept the definition of inflation as a position where prices increase and the value of money depreciates, then the Chancellor's proposals will have an inflationary effect. The additional costs which industry will have to meet as a result of his proposals must, to some extent, be reflected in increased prices. This will, in turn, create a demand for increased incomes to meet them. If he removes the present restrictions on the creation of new money, which are the main reasons for our present lack of economic growth, there is virtually nothing as our system now operates to prevent demands for more money being met.

The regulator we need is one that controls the supply of money and credit at its source. It is ridiculous to suggest that there is no alternative to the tap being either full on or turned completely off. It should be turned on just sufficiently to ensure that the creation of new money and credit is geared to the increase in the production of goods and services. Instead of concentrating all his attention on collecting more money through taxation, the Chancellor would have been wiser to look for a regulator which dealt with the sources of new money.

The suggestion in this letter, that the Chancellor's measures would 'be reflected in increased prices' and that 'this will in turn create a demand for increased incomes' has certainly been proved right in the subsequent period.

When the editor of *The Times* wrote an article proposing a return to a gold standard, I sent the following letter, which was published on 9 May 1974:

Mr Rees-Mogg has rendered a service by raising the question of a return to gold. It is now 50 years since the great controversy on the proposal to return to the gold standard was at its height. A Treasury memorandum accompanying the Gold Standard Bill summarized their reasons for accepting gold: 'Whatever its imperfections, gold for centuries commanded the confidence of the civilized world and has continued to command it. If the gold standard fails to give complete stability, its adoption is nevertheless the most simple and direct method of obtaining a high degree of stability.'

Winston Churchill, then Chancellor of the Exchequer, expressed doubts as to the wisdom of a return to gold. Keynes and McKenna advocated managed money as an alternative, but the combined influence of Montagu Norman, Otto Niemeyer and others proved too strong. Britain return to gold at the prewar parity on April 28, 1925.

But the 'high degree of stability' which the supporters of the gold standard envisaged proved illusory. The deflation which followed proved disastrous, leading to the General Strike of 1926, the spectre of poverty in the midst of plenty, and a total of three million unemployed by 1930. The effects of the poisoning of industrial relations which then took place remain with us to this day.

In the House of Commons on April 21, 1932, Winston Churchill, in the Budget debate, referred to the arguments and forces which had led to the return to gold in 1925. He said: 'Are we really going to accept the position that the whole future development of science, our organization, our increasing cooperation and the fruitful era of peace and goodwill among men and nations; are all these developments to be arbitrarily barred by the price of gold? Is the progress of the human race in this age of almost terrifying expansion to be arbitrarily barred and regulated by fortuitous discoveries of gold mines here and there or by the extent to which we can persuade the existing cornerers and hoarders of gold to put their hoards again into the common stock? Are we to be told that human civilization and society would have been impossible if gold had not happened to be an element in the composition of the globe?'

Mr Rees-Mogg's argument that a gold base for money supplies a much needed discipline on the structure of credit is undoubtedly true. But need we have recourse to such an arbitrary discipline which is unrelated to the needs of the economy? Surely reality and stability demand that money should not be related to one commodity — gold — but to a wide range of commodities. As long ago as 1920 Irving Fisher proposed that the United States should adopt a 'commodity dollar'. Since then there have been many advocates of this idea. Instead of going back to a gold standard, we should be moving forward to a commodity standard, with money based on the goods and services which alone give money its value.

The Times leading article on 6 July 1974 gave another opportunity to write — the letter was published on 11 July 1974.

The Search for a Programme to Stop Inflation

Your splendid leader today (July 6th) gives hope that even at this late hour policies may be introduced which can slow down and eventually halt inflation and thus make possible our national recovery.

The crisis situation which is developing so acutely arises from wrong policies which have been initiated by successive governments and their advisers. There is nothing inherently wrong with the British economy which cannot be put right by the adoption of policies based on common-sense instead of party dogma.

Five years ago we initiated a Programme for National Recovery sponsored by 18 industrialists and economists. After a most careful study of the available statistical information we came to conclusions which can be summarized as follows.

(1) As inflation arises primarily from an expansion of the money supply, monetary policy should be recognized as the key to preventing further inflation. The amount of 'new' money allowed to come into circulation should be limited to the increase in the Gross National Product.

(2) This means that Government expenditure both central and local on current and capital account should be reduced and not allowed to exceed an agreed percentage (say 35 per cent) of the GNP. Public Sector expenditure should then only be allowed to increase in relation to the growth of the private sector.

(3) Fiscal policy should be more closely geared to the provision of incentives to those who produce wealth so that output per person is increased and the total output of productive industry increased.

(4) Restrictive practices whether by employer or employee should be progressively diminished.

(5) Disincentives for people to provide for themselves should be removed.

(6) Saving should be encouraged by providing an inflation proof bond, carrying a Government guarantee against continued inflation with a relatively low rate of interest.

(7) An all-out educational programme should be undertaken to bring home to people that their standard of living depends on the amount of wealth actually produced and that increased money

incomes which are not related to increased production of wealth only increased the cost of living with consequent debasement of the monetary unit.

In April 1976 I returned to a subject which had always interested me, but on which I had never succeeded in getting any satisfaction from official quarters — the way that money is created as an interest-bearing debt.

The following letter appeared in *The Financial Times* on 5 April 1976:

Servicing the National Debt

It has been estimated that the painful economies in the field of public expenditure are likely to be wiped out by the estimated increase in the real burden of debt services. The White Paper on Public Expenditure comments — 'The cost of servicing the debt has risen substantially and because of the cumulative effect of borrowing seems likely to continue to rise in the next few years'.

In this connection, should we not look more closely at the different approach which prevails in regard to the issue of the two main forms of money, the note issue and the issue of credit? In the case of the former, issued by the Bank of England, profits accrue to the national Exchequer, thus providing an interest-free and debt-free issue of money. On the other hand credit, borrowed from the banking system, is issued as a debt carrying interest at the prevailing rate.

As long ago as 1943, an article on 'The Future of Banking' in *The Economist* stated: 'The only justification that can be advanced for charging anything like commercial rates on created credit lent to the Government is that banks incur costs in handling the deposits to which their loan give rise. But if depositors bore the cost of handling this argument would disappear.'

It is legitimate to ask whether, to the extent that credit is created by the banking system to lend to the Government, a payment for the service rendered would not be sounder and more equitable from the national viewpoint? When the Government requires new money to bridge the gap between receipts and expenditure there is, I suggest, no good reason why the nation should be required to pay vast sums in interest charges to the banking system for providing what is, in effect, a service. The same principle should apply, to the creation of the nation's credit as applies to the note issue.

There is no doubt that the banking system provides an invaluable service for which they should be adequately reimbursed. Payment of interest is, in my view, unjustified. No question of savings arise, no-one forgoes claims to wealth and in the true sense of the word, it is not a question of borrowing. The time has come for the Government to re-examine this question and to adopt a more realistic approach to the provision of finances for national purposes before we drown in a sea of unpayable debt.

On this occasion there was a very useful follow-up in the *Financial Times*, for on 12 April 1976 the Lombard Column, then contributed by C. Gordon Tether, took up the question in an article entitled 'Bank Charges — the wider issue', in which he gave notable support to the importance of the issues raised in my letter.

Again in April 1976 I was afforded a splendid opportunity to return to my theme on the subject of the regulation of the money supply. Mr Peter Jay, then Economics Editor of *The Times*, had published an article in which he proposed the setting up of an independent Currency Commission, an idea which I had long advocated. On 26 April 1976 *The Times* published the following letter on this subject:

Regulating the money supply

Your Economics Editor, Mr Peter Jay, has performed an invaluable service in publicizing (*Business News*, April 15) his proposal that an independent Currency Commission should be appointed to regulate the growth of the money supply, relating this to growth in the productive potential of the economy. There is no doubt in my mind that this proposal, if adopted, would do more to establish equilibrium in the economy than any other single act. In the last 50 years we have had experience of the money supply being controlled by a banking system which led to deflation and by the government, which has led to inflation. It is clear that neither is to be trusted to maintain the correct flow of money which would ensure the maintenance of a stable internal general price level and thus prevent both inflation or deflation.

It is interesting to recall that this question was debated in the last century. David Ricardo, recognized as one of the leading thinkers of his day, was responsible for suggesting such a commission in his

Plan for the establishment of a National Bank, published in 1824, a year after his death. He proposed that the right of issue should be returned to the state but that it should be exercised on their behalf by a body of commissioners. He refused to allow the government to have anything to do with it, insisting that the commissioners should be completely independent. He wrote: 'I propose also to prevent all intercourse between these Commissioners and Ministers by forbidding every species of money transaction between them. The Commissioner should never, on any pretence, lend money to the Government, nor be in the slightest degree under its control or influence.'

Sir Robert Peel admitted in a Cabinet memorandum that he approved of Ricardo's plan. He wrote: 'A Board would be constituted, independent of the Government, but responsible to Parliament, charged with the issue of paper, convertible into gold, to be legal tender. If we were about to establish in a new state of society a new system of currency it would be difficult to contest theoretically the principles on which this plan is founded or the equity of the practical application of them.'

Unfortunately, with the passing of the Bank Charter Act in 1844, the proposal was lost. Nearly 150 years later we should have learned that Ricardo was right and that neither bankers nor politicians should be responsible for the control of money supply. This function, as Mr Jay says, should be reserved for a specially appointed body, free from interference from interested parties. There should be no difficulty in finding men and women of the right calibre for this task.

Subsequently, Aims for Freedom and Enterprise published a paper I had written entitled *Honest Money — the Case for a Currency Commision*, which had a wide circulation and received some publicity in the press and on the radio.

The Times published what I believe to be a very important letter on 10 November 1978:

Fundamental Error in Notion that Money Itself has Intrinsic Value

The argument between the so-called monetarists and those who support an incomes policy seems to me to ignore a fundamental error in our thinking about money. People have been brought up to believe that money is itself something of intrinsic value. Though this was at one time true, it is no longer valid. For many years the value of the pound has depended on one thing only — what it will buy. Yet there has been a complete failure to convey this fact to the general public. Hence, we get strikes in support of demands for more money, the result of which is a diminution in the real wealth available, so that finally more money buys less. To give a worker £100 when there is only £50 worth of goods to buy with it merely reduces the purchasing power of the £100 to £50. That is inflation.

It is the failure of successive Governments to recognize this, and the fact that they have pumped more money into circulation regardless of the production of real wealth which has led people to believe that their spending could continue to rise without let or hindrance. The post-war attitude towards monetary policy was well illustrated by the statement in the Radcliffe Report on Credit and Currency published in 1959. It stated: 'Spending is not limited by the amount of money in existence, but it is related to the amount of money people think they can get hold of.' Trade Unionists have obviously taken this to heart!

Having given many years of study to this problem my two main conclusions are as follows:

1. Reality and stability demand that money and goods should be linked together; and that the way to do this is to base money on goods and services, just as we formerly based it on gold or silver. Thus we would introduce a Commodity Standard, money being based on real wealth, i.e, goods and services of all kinds. This would appear to be a logical step in the evolution of money through the ages.

2. The appointment of a monetary authority, free from party political and other pressures, to regulate the growth of money supply to ensure the continued stability of the monetary unit. If the authority regulated the flow of new money in accordance with the volume of real wealth, the outward and visible sign of their success would be the maintenance of the stability of the internal price level. The price index would be the most important guide, indicating the need for alteration in the money supply.

Inflation is a disease: it creates a condition of mind which causes otherwise rational people to behave irrationally. This, I suggest, will continue until the basic facts about money and inflation are made clear and the myth destroyed that money is itself wealth.

This I firmly believe lies at the root of much that has gone wrong and continues to go wrong in our economy.

In an effort to focus attention on the destructive policies being followed by trades unions, I sent the following letter to the *Daily Telegraph*, which was published on March 17, 1979, with a follow-up in August published in the *Daily Telegraph* on 29 August 1979:

The Wealth Destroyers

Sir James Pitman (March 14) rightly points out that trades unions fail to recognize the importance of creating wealth 'because there existed somewhere a cornucopia of great wealth that had been robbed from the employees by their employers and by the Establishment.'

If we look rather more deeply into the reasons for this irrational belief, we must return to the traumatic experiences of the deflationary period.

In the late 1920s and early 1930s, while malnutrition was rife, food and goods of all kinds were being destroyed and their production restricted. So there was, at the time, some sense in the demand for increased purchasing power to enable people to buy what was produced. But it led to the belief that the solution to the problem was to increase purchasing power, ignoring the fundamental fact that an increase in the supply of money unrelated to the production of real wealth, i.e. goods and services of all kinds, simply results in inflation.

The absurdity of the present situation is that while the main aim of the trade union movement is to enhance the standard of living of its members, its actions only result in the lowering of living standards of the entire community including its members. The result of a strike to get more money is inevitably a diminution in the amount of real wealth available.

We must set about the task of making it clear that it is the reverse of common sense to demand more money and at the same time resist by every means the increased production of real wealth.

We are wasting our resources by overmanning and resistance to new techniques. We fail to give worth-while incentives to those who are prepared to work efficiently; at the same time we reward the work-shy. We deny free enterprise.

Free enterprise, given proper incentives could revolutionise our productive capacity. Yet it has been subject to more sustained political attack than in any other industrial nation of the Western world. Excessive taxes have discouraged investment and are turning Britain, once renowned for its honesty, into a nation of tax-dodgers.

The endless debilitating strikes in major industries have undermined our confidence. It is time our union leaders realised that they should resolve inter-union problems by negotiation; they should co-operate with industry to ensure that it makes a profit and can afford to pay higher wages. Instead of demanding increased Government expenditure, they should insist on a reduction with consequent relief in levels of taxation. Increased prosperity would make possible higher real wages to be paid and would make it possible to finance expansion.

This is a year of decision. If we make the right choices, we can look forward to a better life for all; the alternative is disaster.

Will the Unions ever Learn?

Mr Walter Goldsmith, Director-General of the Institute of Directors is right to stress that the task of securing better pay and conditions for their members is the legitimate function of the trade union leadership.

It should, therefore, be asked: When will the trade union leaders recognise the truth of this and begin to actively encourage their members to play a full part in getting the nation back on its feet?

Their present policies, which frequently result in retarding the production of wealth, should give way to positive policies of increasing wealth production. Only thus can the higher standard of living to which they aspire be achieved.

The prime object of the Government must be to conquer inflation, and this must, after such a long period of decline in the purchasing power of the pound, be a painful process. Nevertheless, unless this is achieved, there is no hope of economic recovery.

Inflation is basically caused by the creation of too much money in relation to the volume of goods and services available. There are two main ways of halting inflation. One is to decrease the supply of money. The other, which is more important but is less often realised, is to increase the supply of goods and services.

That it is well within our capacity to increase the flow of real wealth is not in doubt. The under-use of resources, the over-manning in industry and the public services, the failure to use new techniques, are all signs that the working population could if they really understood the basic economic facts, make a marked contribution to solving our problems.

Unfortunately the Government has so far failed to get over the message to the public that the best way to cure inflation is by increasing production and making full use of our resources.

The *Telegraph* allowed me to return once again to the question of regulating the money supply in a letter they published on 15 October 1979:

Regulating the Money Supply

The pledge given by Sir Geoffrey Howe, that the Government will not make a U-turn on its strict monetary control policy is to be sincerely welcomed.

There is one aspect of this policy which, I believe, requires more urgent examination than has so far been given to it.

I refer to the policy of imposing penal rates of interest throughout the economy by increasing minimum lending rate.

This has the effect of automatically increasing interest rates right through the financial system. Interest charged by the banks and other financial institutions is automatically raised and this has harmful effects, not only to the productive element of the economy, but also to the Government's own costs of borrowing, with the added fact that such increased costs help to fuel inflation.

The main reason for the increase in MLR is to act as a brake on the banking system in creating too much money. A more efficient method of regulating money supply is vitally necessary as an essential part of the fight against inflation.

A reference to past experience is, perhaps, not out of place. When war broke out in 1939, the Bank Rate (which preceded MLR) was automatically doubled from 2 per cent to 4 per cent, in line with orthodox policy.

A small but determined group of MPs of all parties together with economists associated with the Economic Reform Club brought pressure to bear on both the Bank of England and the Government to reduce Bank Rate to 2 per cent.

As a result of their success the nation as a whole was saved a vast amount in interest charges on the huge amounts which had to be borrowed to finance the war.

Is it too much to hope that an equally determined and informed group of MPs will take up the challenge and insist that the authorities find a more satisfactory way of regulating money supply and thus reduce the cost of borrowing from its present penal levels?

In February 1980 I returned to the attack in an attempt to inform the trades unions of the true facts of the situation which the *Telegraph* published on 20 February 1980:

Road to Recovery

It is distressing, to say the least, to see and to hear sincere trade union leaders like Mr Bill Sirs constantly demanding 'more money on the table' supported by rank and file members chanting, 'what do we want — 20 per cent.'

It should be asked: What do they really mean? Do they want more pieces of paper to stuff in their wallets, or do they want more purchasing power to enable them and their families to buy more goods and services? If the latter, then their actions belie their words.

The fact is if the time, energy and effort given to prevent the production of real wealth were to be spent on the shop floor increasing the output of goods, then there is little doubt that output would increase in which case they would be fully entitled to their 20 per cent.

The tragedy is in present circumstances, that even if they succeed in getting 'more money on the table' the purchasing power of that money will be still further eroded by falling output of real wealth. It is this failure to recognise that money is not itself wealth, but only a claim to goods and services which alone gives money its value, that lies at the root of much of our current industrial problems.

In Research Paper No. 5 published in 1967 under the auspices of our National Recovery Programme we examined the use of resources in Britain and we concluded that we have a massive potential for economic growth if we were to make full use of our existing resources.

We suggested that Britain could easily achieve a growth of 6½ per cent a year within a few years if we fully used our capacity to create wealth.

Would it not be a worthwhile exercise for the Government to tell the country what could be achieved if we changed our attitude to the creation of wealth? This could be a welcome antidote to the prevailing pessimism about the future.

The comments in the press on the Brandt Commission on North–South relations prompted me to return to the theme of my 1947 broadcast, and *The Times* gave pride of place to my letter on this subject on 16 February 1980:

Plans for the Welfare of the World

In your leading article today (February 13) dealing with the Brandt Commission on North–South relations, you rightly say that the report 'does not wholly face the problem that massive transfers of resources to the South would inevitably mean massive financing of deficits in those areas'.

There is no doubt that this is one of the major factors inhibiting the solution to the problems of the have-not nations. It is being increasingly recognized that some way of dealing with the imbalances arising from the disparity in wealth and natural resources between the developing and developed world is an urgent necessity.

This problem was recognized as urgent in the 1940s, when postwar plans for international trade were under consideration. In 1942, Lord Keynes put forward a scheme which made the point that equal pressure should be brought to bear, not only on the debtor nation to pay its debts, but also on the creditor to accept payment.

Keynes envisaged the setting up of a clearing union where payments between nations could be swopped and the means established to iron out the debtor–creditor relationships. This plan was turned down at Bretton Woods in 1944; it was found unacceptable by the United States Congress of those days.

In 1941 a publication entitled *A Twentieth Century Economic System* was published by the Economic Reform Club and Institute. This envisaged a system of multilateral contra-account, whereby nations would acquire credits in an international clearing union when they exported. It could only clear those credits when it imported, so creating a contra-account. It would not have to import from the country to which it sold but, if it wished to take payment, it could do so only by importing from some other nation to the value of its exports (visible and invisible).

Failure to import would result in a credit held by the international clearing union; credits so created would have an agreed life and would then be cancelled.

This plan, very briefly summarized, achieved significant support at a subsequent conference of Commonwealth Chambers of Commerce and when I broadcast on the subject in 1947 (subsequently published in *The Listener*) letters in support came from all parts of the world.

A similar scheme was put forward by Dr Herbert Feis, at that time an official of the American Treasury. He advocated setting up an international clearing house where claims between the various countries could be swopped and, if claims remained outstanding over an agreed period of years, they could be cancelled.

With the breakdown of the Bretton Woods system, the need for a better system of international payments is increasingly recognized. A system under which nations in credit should accept the obligation, which is now crucial in the case of the developing countries, to increase the volume of their imports would give the debtors the opportunity of meeting their indebtedness. Such a system would provide the machinery whereby export surplus and deficit balances were held is an agreed clearing union.

The high-income industrialized countries need an expansion of world markets. The low-income countries would provide the capacity for that expansion if means were found to enable them to meet their obligations without being saddled with unpayable debt.

Aid and loans cannot by themselves do more than tinker with this problem. I suggest we need to re-examine the ideas put forward in the 1940s as a matter of supreme urgency.

On 6 March 1980 *The Times* published a further attempt to set the record straight on the question of deflation and inflation:

Economic Lessons from 1930s

In the current debate on Britain's road to hyper-inflation there are some lessons to be learned from the 1930s. Fifty years ago the problem was deflation, not inflation. Following the return to the gold standard in 1925, the amount of money in circulation was reduced. By 1930 there were nearly three million unemployed, there was a steady appreciation in the value of money, prices fell, often below the costs of production, bringing bankruptcy and ruin to many producers of wealth. We were told to 'tighten our belts' and had to accept a 10 per cent cut in incomes and a reduced standard of living.

At the same time the country was full of unsaleable goods, foodstuffs rotted in the ground, milk was poured down drains while children were undernourished. Typical headlines in the press of those days were 'Enough wheat to last for two years', 'Coffee burned by the ton', 'More tea than we can drink'.

The *Sunday Express* commented: 'The world is full to the overflowing with the greatest surplus of goods in history.' In a search for the remedy for this dilemma described as 'poverty in the midst of plenty' the economists and financial experts (with some notable exceptions) searched in vain for the answer to the problem. They looked everywhere except in the realm of a deflationary monetary policy where the true reason was to be found. Those who urged that more money should be put into circulation to enable people to buy what was already available were dismissed as monetary cranks.

What is the relevance of this to the present situation? The answer is to be found in the fact that since 1945 successive governments have reversed pre-war policy by pumping more money into circulation without regard to the increase in the quantity of goods and services available to be consumed. As in a deflationary monetary policy the value of the monetary unit appreciates, so with an inflationary monetary policy the value of the monetary unit depreciates. Both are wrong and the results are calamitous.

Those who refuse to admit the importance of money supply in the inflationary situation are guilty of the same error as those who refused to recognize that the pre-war deflation was also a monetary phenomenon.

In her speech in Parliament yesterday (February 28) the Prime Minister made an important pronouncement, she said: 'Experience shows that the only way of attacking inflation is to keep the money supply closely related to the output of goods and services. Whenever governments have not followed this simple rule — when money is in greater supply than goods — inflation has resulted.'

I returned to the idea of a Currency Commission in a letter published in the *Financial Times* on the following day, 7 March:

A Currency Commission

I was interested to see Samuel Brittan's reference in the Lombard column (March 3) to the proposal for the establishment of an independent currency commission made by Mr Peter Jay in April 1976. This idea had been put forward by leading economists over the past 200 years. For example, David Ricardo in the early 19th century wrote of the need for the appointment of a currency commission which should be a completely independent body. Robert Torrens gave support to Ricardo's plan which commended itself to Sir Robert Peel.

In the early part of this century Professor Irving Fisher of Yale University proposed a currency commission which should be empowered to issue the money of the nation to regulate it in accordance with a legal criterion of stabilisation. In this country Professor Frederick Soddy, a Nobel prizeman whose contribution to monetary problems has never been fully recognized, argued for 'a purely scientific statistical authority, analogous to the institutions charged with the control of weights and measures, but preferably directly under the Crown, to determine the rate at which new national money is to be issued in order to maintain the price-index of the main commodities invariable'. There is no doubt that had these proposals been implemented, serious inflation would have been impossible.

It is worth recalling that when we went off the gold standard in 1931, an Exchange Equalisation Account was set up, charged with the main task of stabilising the external value of the £ sterling. Had the authorities then also set up a currency commission charged with the task of maintaining the stability of the internal general price level, subsequent history would have been very different. The appointment of a currency commission, free from party political and other pressures would play an important part in preventing both inflation and deflation, from which we have suffered so grievously in the past 50 years.

A letter criticising the case for a currency commission from John Mills was published on 21 March and on 8 April the *Financial Times* published the following reply:

Deflation and Inflation

Mr John Mills (March 21) challenges the case made in my letter of March 7 for the establishment of a Currency Commission. He asserts that 'the collapse in 1929 had nothing to do with money supply'. In fact, it was the failure of the Federal Reserve to carry out its task of maintaining the liquidity of the US banking system which was the main factor in the subsequent collapse.

The depression in the UK, however, had started prior to 1929, the return to the gold standard in 1925 started a deflationary trend, culminating in nearly 3m unemployed by 1930. The outward and visible sign of this deflation, clearly shown below, was the appreciation in the purchasing power of the £, accompanied by wholesale destruction and restriction in the production of food and goods.

Since 1945 a steady erosion in the purchasing power of the £ has taken place, as shown below. This is the outward and visible sign of inflation, which has, of course, worsened considerably since 1970.

The aim of monetary policy should be to maintain the liquidity of the monetary system at such a volume that the general price level is held constant, which we have signally failed to do since 1914. If a Currency Commission, charged with the task of maintaining the stability of the purchasing power of the £ had been in existence, it could, I suggest, have played a significant part in preventing pre-war deflation and post-war inflation and stop-go policies by ensuring that the money supply was closely related to the output of goods and services.

DEFLATION AND INFLATION IN BRITAIN 1914-70

	s	d	
1914	20	0	1914–20: Wartime inflation
1920	8	0	
1925	11	5	1925: Deflation (gold standard)
1930	12	8	
1935	14	0	1935–40: Reflation
1940	10	3	1940–45: Wartime inflation
1945	7	10	
1950	6	3	1950–70: Postwar inflation
1955	5	0	
1960	4	6	
1965	3	11	
1970	2	6	

More recently I have written a number of letters to the national press on the subject of Government Debt and Credit Creation, the subject of our most recent publication. In the main these have been turned down, which seems to point that the subject is not one which commends itself to those who control the media. However, after several abortive attempts to overcome this embargo, *The Guardian* published the following letter on Tuesday, 29 January 1985:

Creating Credit that could be Spent on Producing Jobs
Your Leader 'Wriggling in a vortex of decline' (January 23) points out that 'interest on Government debt is the fastest rising of

all areas of public spending; it has grown from £3.4 billion in 1979/80 to £8.5 billion this year.'

At this rate of progression it will not be many years before the entire taxable capacity of the country is required to meet this liability. Yet you say 'we need a sharp increase in spending to produce wealth and jobs.' How can these two contrary needs to reduce debt and ensure expansion be met? To solve this dilemma, we need to look at the way the bulk of new money comes into circulation as a debt, bearing interest. By a curious anomaly, money in the form of notes — a small percentage of total money supply — is issued through the Bank of England, the profits on issue accruing to the Treasury.

But credit is created by the banking system and issued as a debt-bearing interest. Thus, when the Government borrows from the banking system, it thereby increases the debt burden.

The interest which has to be paid by the Treasury to the banking system when additional sums are required for financing Government expenditure, accounts for a substantial proportion of Government spending.

Is there a way round this problem? In a publication, Government Debt and Credit Creation, we have attempted to show that it would be possible to increase spending to produce wealth and jobs if the Government were to adopt the same principle to the creation of credit as applies to the note issue.

18

THE SWING OF THE PENDULUM

It was in the early part of 1981 that I began to question whether the economic policies which the Conservative government were following were producing the right results. To some extent the government was at least attempting to follow the ideas we had put forward in our National Recovery Programme and other publications — that taxation was too high; that government expenditure must be contained; that interest rates needed to be reduced. Yet it was increasingly obvious that they were not succeeding. Taxation remained too high, the government continued to take too high a proportion of the national income and rates of interest remained high. Worst of all, unemployment continued to rise to unacceptable levels. The rate of growth in the economy was abysmal and the nation's economy was far from being in a healthy condition.

The one area where success could be claimed was the reduction of inflation, but the price of the turn-round had been very great. The question inevitably arose — had the pendulum swung too far from inflation to deflation? There were uncomfortable signs that the nation was once again seeing the return to the deflation of the 1930s with unused resources of manpower and idle capacity in industry. The authorities were relying on encouraging the development of a free market economy, but failing to recognise that a free market economy could only function properly if the monetary system truly reflected facts and facilitated both production and consumption. Something was obviously wrong and lacking in the government's economic and monetary strategy if the unused resources of manpower and productive capacity could not be utilised to develop the infrastructure, including areas of health, transport and roads,

166

education, housing etc., which were badly in need of investment.

It was in these circumstances that in the 1930s John Maynard Keynes' powerful intellect caused him to challenge the orthodox views of the day. He argued that at a time of recession, public expenditure should be increased so as to increase employment, raise spending power and stimulate investment and production. In fact, he recognised clearly that such action should only be taken when unused resources were available. He certainly would not have advocated increasing the quantity of money in times of scarcity as the following quotation from his book *How to Pay for the War* shows:

> What is fairly obvious to common sense, that in a war like this the amount of goods available for consumption will have to be diminished, — and certainly cannot be increased above what it was in peace time.
>
> It follows that the increased quantity of money available to be spent in the pockets of consumers will meet a quantity of goods which is not increased. Unless we establish iron regulations limiting what is to be sold and establishing maximum prices for every article of consumption, with the result that there is nothing left to buy and the consumer goes home with the money burning in his pocket, there are only two alternatives. Some means must be found for withdrawing purchasing power from the market; or prices must rise until the available goods are selling at figures which absorb the increased quantity of expenditure, — in other words the method of inflation.

I observed that we are witnessing a situation when deficit spending on the lines advocated by Keynes could be beneficial but the difficulty which arises in advocating increased government spending is that to the extent it 'borrows' money from the banking system, which is the main source of additional money (credit) supply, it thereby fuels inflation through the multiplier effect described later in this chapter.

These questions were uppermost in our minds when, with a colleague, Simon Webley, a fellow-member of the Executive of the Economic Research Council, we were discussing these problems at a lunch at the Institute of Economic Affairs.

During this discussion we got on to the need to examine the way the government financed its expenditure and in particular, on the way it borrowed credit from the banking system on which it had to pay interest. This harked back to the case made during the war in the series of pamphlets under the title 'The Banks and the War'. To summarise the argument then put forward: 'It is apparent that no new [credit] money can be created except through the banking system, which issues it as an interest-bearing debt. The result of this has been the piling up of an enormous burden of debt on which succeeding generations of our people will have to pay huge sums each year in the form of interest and Sinking Fund.'

Shortly after this I met two colleagues of former years who had been active in the New Britain Movement, Harry Rutherford and David Shillan. They had both worked with Professor Soddy in the past and as a result were very fully informed on the subject of monetary reform. They were both strongly of the opinion that the time had come to make a further effort to get this subject ventilated and Harry Rutherford indicated that he might be able to raise some funds towards the cost of the necessary research.

Encouraged by this, I decided to put the proposition of a research project on the subject of money and credit creation to Damon de Laszlo who had succeeded his father, Patrick de Laszlo, as Chairman of the Economic Research Council. I found that his own mind had been working in the same direction and he agreed to put up some of the necessary funds to finance the project. We obtained the agreement of the Executive Committee of the Council and commissioned Malcolm Macdonald, who had already carried out some very valuable research for us, to undertake this further task.

Thus, we set in motion the study which we finally published in December 1981 under the title *Government Debt and Credit Creation — a study of the creation of credit and its effect on the British economy*. Following previous experience we arranged a press conference, but here we struck a serious snag. With our previous publications, we had always had a representative selection of journalists who attended our press conferences and had given our case an acceptable coverage in the national press.

On this occasion, in spite of having the assistance of a publicity assistant who had publicised the conference, no press and only one representative of the BBC joined us. He began by being very critical, but after about an hour of very full discussion, he agreed that it was worth further consideration. He therefore recorded an interview which we understood would be broadcast in a BBC radio programme shortly afterwards. In the event, the interview was not broadcast and equally, our publication was ignored by the national press, though Sir Arthur Bryant wrote two articles in his column in the *Illustrated London News* which gave us his full support. So far as we were able to ascertain, the only other reference to the publication was made some time afterwards by Gordon Tether in *The Times*, shortly before his column was discontinued. I wrote a number of letters to the national press which attempted to summarise our findings in the study, but all were turned down with the usual plea of lack of space. This does seem to support the theory put forward by the late Professor Soddy, that there is a 'conspiracy of silence' on this whole subject of money creation. I recall some years ago when I was invited to provide a script to the BBC on the subject 'Where Money Comes From'. Having submitted a script which I thought was simplicity itself, it was turned down as being too complicated.

In spite of this virtual blackout on publicity for the case we had put forward, the booklet began to circulate among our members and to a wider public as a result of our own efforts to publicise it. We devoted one of our dinner meetings to the subject and though there were some who differed, we had a very useful interchange of views.

We attempted to get our friends in Parliament to take an interest. Sir John Biggs-Davison put down a Question to the Chancellor which after some delay received a very noncommittal reply. Sir John Eden also took up the matter with the Treasury and a more detailed reply came from Jock (now Lord) Bruce-Gardyne, which did not get to grips with our main contention. We took the matter up with him, and in his reply he did attempt to deal with our proposals but stated that 'I do see substantial objections to what you propose.' Perhaps the most revealing comment was 'an obligation on the banks to hold noninteresting-bearing paper in excess of the amount they choose to hold for transactions purposes would entail a fundamental change in the relationship between government and the banks, of a kind the Government would not wish to contemplate'.

Failure to get any further advance in consideration of our proposals and the obvious dilemma of the government in their efforts to stay within the public sector borrowing requirement encouraged us to send the following letter to the Chancellor of the Exchequer, having first ensured that it would be personally drawn to his attention:

The Rt. Hon. N. Lawson, M.P.,
Chancellor of the Exchequer,
11 Downing Street, London SW1.

13th July 1983

Dear Chancellor,

The fact that you have been constrained to introduce an emergency package of £1,000m of spending cuts and unspecified state assets sales, and the possibility of a cut in aggregate Government spending in 1984–85, has aroused some concern, even among your own supporters. We appreciate the need for the Government to stay within public sector borrowing requirement targets but would draw your attention to one area of expenditure which seems to have escaped attention. That is the interest which has to be paid by the Treasury to the banking system when additional sums are required for financing Government expenditure.

It is a strange anomaly that money in the form of the note issue is created mainly by the Bank of England, the amount being fixed in agreement with the Treasury. The interest earned on the securities held by the Bank of England Issue Department against the issue of notes is refunded to the Treasury since the Bank of England is a Government Agent and profits on its operations are payable to the Treasury.

We suggest that more use could be made of the note issue and that this area along with the creation of credit by the banking system should be further researched. The power of the banks to increase the amount of *credit* money in circulation should revert to the State where historically it belongs. Had this been done, we have estimated some £30,000m could have been saved by the Government since 1945 if they had maintained their historic privilege of themselves issuing all forms of money, *including credit* which is now the main component of the money stock.

We submit that, as the banking system in creating credit is merely using the Nation's credit by liquefying it, the right of the banks to treat such created credit as a loan and to receive payments of interest thereon is unjustified, though they are fully entitled to an agreed fee based on extra work devolving upon them.

Savings achieved by the adoption of these ideas could have substantially reduced the borrowing requirement and would have assisted in the fight against inflation which we agree is a major requirement of Government policy.

Yours sincerely,

D. P. DE LASZLO   EDWARD HOLLOWAY
Chairman   *Hon. Secretary*

After a very long delay we finally received an answer from the Economic Secretary, in which he said:

> The Economic Secretary has asked me to thank you for and to reply to your letter of 13th July 1983. The Economic Secretary was grateful for your agreement about the need for the Government to stay within the forecast public sector borrowing requirement but he does not accept your analysis of the nature of credit creation and the role of the banking system. He regrets therefore that he cannot agree with your proposal.

As we commented at the time, it seems strange that a Government which is so committed to a reduction in government spending and is currently seeking every way of cutting expenditure seems to ignore the one area where, as is shown in *Government Debt and Credit Creation*, there are substantial savings to be made.

By the end of 1983 the results of the efforts made by members of the Council to bring our proposals to the attention of their MPs began to bear fruit, and in January 1984 we were able to make the following progress report:

A Progress Report

by Damon de Laszlo, Chairman of the Economic Research Council

When the ERC launched the above research report in December 1981, it sank, but not without trace. Probably the complexity of the subject and the fact that very few people were concerned with the National Debt at that time, made it less than popular reading just before Christmas.

However, due to a great deal of persistence by a number of our members, the subject has over the last two years started to raise interest. In particular, Mr William Armstrong and Mr Geoffrey Leese — two members in Scarborough — persuaded their Member of Parliament, Sir Michael Shaw, that it was a worthy subject to be presented to the Conservative Backbench Finance Committee in the House of Commons.

It is with great pleasure that I have to report that Edward Holloway and I made this presentation on the evening of 24th January. It was a presentation that filled me with trepidation, as the Committee has extremely knowledgeable members. After the presentation of our case, we were asked a lot of very deep and probing questions for half-an-hour. At the end of the exercise, I feel we managed to stir up a great deal of interest in the subject — probably the most important result being that a number of influential Members of Parliament are now much more concerned about the rate at which the National Debt is compounding, and accept that the subject needs careful scrutiny. The Chairman of the Committee, Sir William Clark, wrote after the meeting: 'Everybody was delighted with the speech and the way you handled the questions afterwards.'

In a different area, John Moore, M.P., Financial Secretary to the Treasury, very kindly lunched with Edward Holloway and me to talk about the subject. We did not expect him to comment on the merit of our argument. However, he was interested enough in the ERC's proposal to ask us to discuss the subject with some of his Treasury technical experts.

Mr Moore commented in a letter: 'We do value the work of independent research bodies such as the Economic Research Council and I hope you will continue to publish original ideas on key current issues.'

Also, during January, we managed to interest Andrew Knight, Editor of the *Economist*, in the subject. There is no way of knowing what the result of the discussions with Mr Knight will be, if any, but at least the *Economist* is not unaware of our existence.

All in all, January 1984 has brought with it the prospect that the subject of Government Debt and Credit Creation will become a live issue.

Following this, R. V. Mummery who lives in Jersey, together with other members of the Council, took the initiative of sending to all Westminster MPs an extract from *Government Debt and Credit Creation*, giving the summary and conclusions of the report and recommending further study. In the covering letter it said: 'The compounding burden of debt threatens to strangle the economic life of the United Kingdom.' It pointed out that in Jersey 'the island Parliament, the States, issues its own interest free currency, we have a lower rate of income tax and no VAT!' Needless to say, the replies received were polite but non-committal. At least no-one challenged the case put forward which is perhaps significant.

In October 1984 I had the opportunity of having a brief conversation with the Prime Minister at a reception in London. Having made this informal contact, I decided to write to her directly, giving my views on the need for reform of monetary policy. I knew that Sir Arthur Bryant had also written personally on the same subject and had received a courteous reply; so on 24 October 1984 I wrote to Mrs Thatcher, asking her if she would consider instituting an enquiry into our proposals. She replied on 14 November as follows:

10 Downing Street

14 November 1984

Dear Mr Holloway,

Thank you for your letter of 24 October on the need for reform of monetary policy and, in particular, the proposal that the Government should take direct control of the issue of credit.

As I said in my letter to Sir Arthur Bryant, I fully share your approach to inflation and high government borrowing. Over the past few years we have made substantial progress in reducing both. Our eventual aim is zero inflation, and we intend to achieve this through firm control of the money supply and public sector borrowing. No system of monetary control is perfect, but our success so far does not suggest that the deficiences of our current system are such as to prevent us meeting these objectives.

Central to our approach has been the desire to remove obstacles to the free operation of market forces in the economy. This is as important in the monetary sector as elsewhere. Bringing the whole process of credit creation under Treasury direction would be a step back towards the sort of quantitative controls on the banking system which produced such damaging distortions in the past. Within a market framework we have to pay the market price for funds that we borrow, if savings are allocated efficiently between the Government and the private sector, as well as within the private sector itself.

I have studied the correspondence the ERC has had with Treasury Ministers since I wrote to Sir Arthur Bryant, and I understand that Damon de Laszlo, your Chairman, has met Treasury Officials to discuss these ideas in detail. We have done our best to do full justice to the ERC's proposals in this area, and I do not see how further work could resolve the fundamental problems I have outlined above. Though I cannot see a place for these particular proposals in the Government's armoury against inflation, I can assure you that I shall continue to use all the means available to achieve our shared objective of sustained non-inflationary growth in a competitive, free market economy.

Yours sincerely,

MARGARET THATCHER

I welcomed this reply, but the phrase 'within a market framework we have to pay the market price for funds' seemed to indicate that the full significance of our proposals for debt-free and interest-free currency had not been fully understood. I therefore decided to send a follow-up letter which referred to measures taken in the war years which I hoped might clarify the position:

ECONOMIC RESEARCH COUNCIL
55 Park Lane
London W1

4th December 1984

Dear Mrs Thatcher,

Thank you very much for replying so fully in your letter of 14 November and for your careful consideration of the points I raised in my letter of 24 October. While I fully share your views on the need to combat inflation, I would urge that we also need to guard against the dangers of deflation, I have vivid memories of the harmful effects of the latter in the 1920's–30's.

The White Paper 'Employment Policy' (Cmd 6527) of May 1944 stated in the foreward '. . . widespread unemployment in this country can be prevented by a policy of maintaining total internal expenditure'. Again in Chapter IV it states 'Total expenditure on goods and services must be prevented from falling to a level where general unemployment appears'. The question is how to achieve this without inflation.

In an effort to seek some way out of the current dilemma my mind went back to the method of financing the 1939–45 war. Fears were then expressed that it would lead to rip-roaring inflation. This did not happen.

There were three main developments which, I believe, prevented this:

1. The replacement of borrowing on Treasury Bills by the Treasury Deposit Receipt.
2. The maintenance of a 2 per cent bank rate.
3. The introduction of the Keynes plan for Post War Credits as an alternative to increased taxation.

The policy of substituting Treasury Deposit Receipts for Treasury Bills was, I suggest, a major factor. As the Bank of England's evidence to the Radcliffe Committee on credit and currency clearly showed; —

'If the Exchequer borrows by issuing Treasury Bills which are taken up by the banks and spends the proceeds (so that the cash borrowed finds its way back to the banks) the liquid assets and deposits of the banks will be increased and they will be put in a position to increase the supply of bank credit.'

Indeed only a proportion of the bank's deposits requires to be covered by cash and other liquid assets; a given loss or gain of liquid assets by the banks has an effect several times as great on the potential volume of bank credit.'

It was here that the T.D.R's played a significant role as they could not be used as part of the banks liquid assets on which additional credits could be created. Thus they were not in a position to increase the volume of bank credit by several times which would have been the case with the Treasury Bill. Could not this be applied to part of the P.S.B.R. as an experiment?

The second factor was that Bank Rate was held at 2 per cent for the war period. On the outbreak of war it was doubled to 4 per cent, but an all-party group of M.P's, with whom I was associated, brought pressure on the authorities and got it reduced.

The third point which might be worthy of consideration in present circumstances is the plan for Post War Credits. As you know, this enabled the Exchequer to keep taxation at a lower level than would otherwise have been the case. Introduced today as an 'INVEST IN BRITAIN' scheme, it might well be acceptable if it helped reduce taxation. It would have the added attraction if it was introduced as part of the plan to extend share ownership, for the tax credits could allow for a dividend to be paid to the holders in line with the growth of the economy. It is an idea capable of variation but it might well appeal to people's patriotism in present circumstances.

Yours sincerely,
EDWARD HOLLOWAY

The reply came a few days later, signed by Andrew Turnbull, Private Secretary:

10 Downing Street

11 December 1984

Dear Mr Holloway,

Thank you for your letter to the Prime Minister of 4 December to which I have been asked to reply. You raised a number of interesting points about the conduct of monetary policy and the instruments used in the period immediately after the war. While the Government shares fully your objective of securing growth without inflation, it believes that the monetary conditions needed for this can be achieved within the present structure of the banking system and by using existing instruments of monetary policy.

Yours sincerely,
Andrew Turnbull

Following this unsatisfactory exchange of views with the Prime Minister and Treasury we had some discussions with one or two peers, and as a result the following interesting exchange took place in the House of Lords on Tuesday 23 July 1985.

MONETARY POLICY
Questions in the House of Lords

On the questionof Money Supply, Lord Beswick posed the following Question—'To ask Her Majesty's Government whether, in view of the fact that the money supply has increased by 101.9 per cent in the 5-year period to mid-April and that only 5 per cent is accounted for by the increase of state minted coins and the printing of currency notes, they will now state by whom the remaining 96.9 per cent of money was created and under whose authority.'

In reply, the Earl of Gowrie said: 'The additional 96.9 per cent represents new bank deposits, created in the normal course of banking business. No Government Authority is necessary for this.'

Lord Beswick replied: 'I thank the noble Earl for that reply, the implication of which are of course very far reaching. Would the noble Earl not agree that at one time it was clearly understood and firmly enforced that the only authority in the country which was empowered to create money, either by printing notes or minting coins, was the Government of the day, the state? Now that credit transactions have largely superseded minted money and paper currency, is there not some reason for asking for an authoritative and objective commission to consider this matter and to see who is getting the benefit of this enormous amount of extra money that is being created each year?'

The Earl of Gowrie replied: 'The noble Lord makes an interesting suggestion, though, as he has said, for Question Time it is perhaps a little far-reaching in its implications. It seems to me that on the whole the economies of the Western World are benefiting from these new monetary habits.'

Lord Tranmire followed with a supplementary question: 'Are not the figures for the increase in bank credit and money supply disturbing when compared with the annual increase in output of 3 per cent? Will my noble friend have a look at this as suggested by the noble Lord, Lord Beswick, and have an enquiry made into how money and credit come into circulation and the consequent burden of the increase in our national debt as a result.'

To which the Earl of Gowrie replied: 'The Government keep a very close watch on monetary aggregates, as the House would expect. I agree with my noble friend that there have been some rather eccentric movements in M3 recently, but I am glad to tell my noble friend and the Opposition that M0 has been behaving impeccably.'

Lord Barnett asked: 'Can the noble Earl tell us what has been happening to M1, M2, M3, PSL1, PSL2, and PSL3, and which of them the Government think is right?'

The Earl of Gowrie replied: 'The Government think that the monetary aggregate indications of the present rates of inflation are broadly right and are a great deal better than the behaviour of any of the monetary aggregates when the noble Lord was Chief Secretary to the Treasury.'

Lord Bottomley asked: 'Is the noble Lord aware that during the last war Government policy was fully to employ labour and materials to win the war? This was done with a modest increase in inflation. Can the Minister say why the present Government do not follow a similar policy to win the peace?'

Finally, Lord Beswick returned to his original Question: 'Would the noble Earl be good enough to draw a distinction between the Question which I asked and the one asked by my noble friend on the front bench? I am not querying the amount of money that has been created under these different guises. What I am asking is: who is getting the benefit of it? As things are, it would appear that it is the private banking institutions, and not the Government. In view of the fact that the Government have this enormous problem in public sector borrowing, would it not be right to have this matter more carefully assessed?'

The Earl of Gowrie replied: 'Of course I am glad to acquit the noble Lord, Lord Beswick, of low political behaviour. The fact of the matter is that he is sceptical of whether the banking institutions should be the proper sources of supply in this area, and we are less sceptical. As I say, it is a somewhat knotty issue to take up in a question and answer session.'

Following this interchange the House of Lords went on to debate the Finance Bill. The following extract is of interest.

The Earl of Gowrie: 'The American headache is deficit financing—running an overdraft. Most American commentators do not believe that the deficit can be sustained, and yet the American boom depends on it, and before long the American boom may start to wobble. The headache of the developing countries is debt. The scale of their debt may imperil the growth rates of our developed world, growth rates on which they, in turn, depend.'

Present indications are that the government is completely satisfied with its present policies and we can, therefore, only await further developments. At least we can claim that they are aware of the alternative offered by many sincere supporters of the monetary reforms we have so consistently supported.

CONCLUSION

Some years ago Winston Churchill said that mankind was faced with a choice — on the one hand 'Measureless Reward' and on the other, 'Supreme Disaster'. His words were prophetic. Today we witness the final struggle between these two alternatives. Either we accept all the benefits which flow from man's inventiveness and technological progress, or we sink into increasing chaos and disaster. This really summarises the reason why I have devoted so much of my life in an effort to reform the monetary system. No-one pretends that this alone would solve mankind's dilemmas, for as we approach the twenty-first century, enormous problems loom which will take all our efforts to solve. But, in my belief, they can only be solved if we have a really 'honest' money system which reflects real facts on which to base our economic life. Today there is a misconception about money which is wrongly regarded as wealth in itself instead as a claim to real wealth, i.e. goods and services of all kinds. We have learnt to worship money, and in so doing we worship, ignorantly and harmfully, a man-made idol. It is well said that the love of money is the root of all evil.

The struggle to achieve an honest money system has gone on for many years. Abraham Lincoln was very specific on this 'The privilege of creating and issuing money is not only the supreme prerogative of Government, but it is the Government's greatest opportunity' (US Senate Document No.23). Over the years there have been many pronouncements by leading statesmen, scientists and economists who have supported this view. Today there are lively movements in many parts of the world trying to enlighten public opinion and thereby influence governments in their own country. This is particularly true of the United States where groups such as 'Truth in Money' are very active. There is also an increasing awareness on the part of

academics in universities who have given their support to the
need for reform. In Canada, Australia and New Zealand there
are groups of people beavering away in an attempt to overcome
the silence which surrounds the subject in the press and other
organs of the media.

The 'Measureless Reward' to which Sir Winston referred
springs from the revolution which is taking place in the sphere
of the production of wealth. No longer do men and women have
to slave to produce wealth, for, aided by the technological
revolution, mankind can be progressively freed from the need to
work so hard to provide for a full life. John Maynard Keynes, in
his *Essays in Persuasion* (1963), summarises the position
which arises: 'Thus for the first time since his creation man will
be faced with his real, his permanent problem — how to use his
freedom from pressing economic cares, how to occupy his
leisure, which science and compound interest have won for
him, to live wisely, agreeably and well.'

This, then, is the real motivation for my fifty years of effort,
to see established an 'Age of Leisure' when mankind can devote
itself to using its creative capacity to enhance the environment,
to encourage the pursuit of beauty and craftmanship which
enabled previous generations to construct cathedrals and build-
ings of architectural excellence and to enable people to live
'wisely, agreeably and well' and to banish the friction which
causes nations to quarrel. Utopia, perhaps, but everyone is
entitled to a dream!

Can we imagine a world where, instead of unemployment
being regarded as a misfortune, leisure is sought after and
prized for the opportunities it gives to live a full and satisfactory
life? Where education is as much devoted to teaching people to
aim at worthwhile and satisfying leisure occupations as to earning a living? Where nations, removed from the necessity to
'export or die', recognise that the true purpose of international
trade is to enhance the living standards of both buyer and seller?
The remaining years of the twentieth century will decide
whether this is possible, and we all have a responsibility.

I am very conscious that in attempting to set out the background of activity with which I have been associated over the
years I have omitted far more than is included in what of

necessity can be contained in a reasonable compass. In particular, I apologise for not mentioning so many sincere and honest people with whom I have been associated in these endeavours. It is perhaps the greatest reward which has come to me that I have had the privilege of knowing so many splendid characters who have put their own interests on one side for a cause they believed in.

Mankind is at a crossroads: let us pray that it takes the right path.

APPENDIX I

ECONOMIC RESEARCH COUNCIL

61 Montagu Square, London W1H 1TG
Telephone: 01-724 5778

President	The Lord Ezra
Chairman	Damon de Laszlo
Vice-Presidents	The Lord Killearn
	Sir Ian Mactaggart Bt
	Sir Peter Parker LVO
	The Lord Seebohm
Hon. Secretary	Edward Holloway

Membership

Membership of the Economic Research Council is open to all who are in sympathy with its declared objects. The minimum annual subscription for individual members is £10 for full members, £5 associate members.

Corporate membership is open to all companies and other bodies, minimum annual subscription £35 in respect of which they may send up to six nominees to any of the Council's discussion meetings and lectures.

Copies of Annual Report, List of Publications and other information from the Hon. Secretary, Economic Research Council, 61 Montagu Square, London W1H 1TG: telephone 01-724 5778.

Some of the distinguished speakers who have addressed our members at Dinners since 1964.

LORD BOOTHBY	The Crisis and the Way Out
PROFESSOR R. G. HAWTREY	What of an Expansionist Policy?

183

LORD LEVER	Economics of a Social Democrat
PROFESSOR J. E. MEADE	Planning and the Price Mechanism
SIR ROY HARROD	International Liquidity
VICTOR FEATHER	The Role of the Trades Unions in the 1960's
DR DUDLEY STAMP	The Wind of Change in Agriculture
SIR EDWARD BOYLE	The New Regulations
LORD STONHAM	British Agriculture and the Common Market
LORD TWEEDSMUIR	Canada in the 20th Century
HON MAXWELL STAMP	The Problem of International Payments
LORD REITH	State-Owned Corporations
JAMES CALLAGHAN, MP	Prospects for 1964
REGINALD MAUDLING, MP	Full Employment and Economic Stability
ENOCH POWELL, MP	Economic Measures
PROFESSOR NICHOLAS KALDOR	Investment Incentives
SIR GEORGE BOLTON	The Problems of Exchange
LORD BEECHING	Government and Industry
LORD ROBENS	Coal in an Expanding Energy Market
LORD SIEFF	Growth of a Distributive Enterprise
LORD HOUGHTON	'Civilized Selectivity' in Social Benefits
SELWYN LLOYD, MP	Government Expenditure
SIR DAVID BARRAN	Anatomy of a Decision
PROFESSOR G. C. ALLEN	Japan's Economic Growth
PROFESSOR GEOFFREY MAYNARD	Comments on British Economic Policy
SIR JAMES GOLDSMITH	A Critical Look at the Constitutional Structure of Britain
SIR GEOFFREY HOWE, QC, MP	Some Thoughts on Economic Problems
SIR HERMANN BONDI, KCB	Energy Policy
JOHN BIFFEN, MP	Current Economic Problems

C. McMAHON	Aspects of British Economic Policy
SIR JOHN BIGGS-DAVISON, MP	Impressions of Central Africa
LORD SEEBOHM	
PROFESSOR A. A. WALTERS	
SIR KEITH JOSEPH, MP	A Topic of Current Economic Interest
CLIVE JENKINS	The Treasury and the Union Economic Policy
LORD HARRIS of HIGH CROSS	Fallacy of the Mixed Economy
PROFESSOR PATRICK MINFORD	What Policy for Sterling
SIR EDWARD du CANN, MP	Report of the Treasury Select Committee
VISCOUNT TRENCHARD	Plans to Revive the Economy
SIR JOHN GREEN BOROUGH, KBE	Economics and Industry
LEON BRITTAN, QC, MP	Government Economic Strategy
LORD ROLL of IPSDEN	Economics—a Lethal Weapon: Handle Carefully
SIR PETER PARKER	Renaissance of Rail—The Non-Utopian Line
SIR GEORGE JEFFERSON	The Opportunities for the
J. H. HARVEY-JONES	Private Sector of British Industry in the Future
LORD EZRA	The Need for an Industrial Strategy

APPENDIX II   We Beg to Differ

FREE TRADE IN MONEY — OR BI-LATERAL BARTER, A FALSE DILEMMA

The text of a broadcast talk given on 9 September 1947, in the Third Programme of the BBC by Edward Holloway. Reprinted by kind permission of the BBC.

In 1925 — the Government of the day put Britain back on a Gold Standard. In 1932 — Mr Winston Churchill, who as Chancellor of the Exchequer, had been responsible for this decision, told the House of Commons he'd been assured by the highest experts that 'we were anchoring ourselves to reality and stability', and he went on to say that the views of the experts had proved to be completely wrong.

In 1945 — the present Government accepted the Loan from the USA with certain commercial conditions attached, including the acceptance of the Bretton Woods Monetary Agreement. Speaking to the Delegates at the TUC the other day Mr Ernest Bevin confessed that in accepting the Loan 'our calculations were wrong'.

Here are two issues of major economic importance where acceptance of views given by the experts has led the politician into grave difficulties and the people into much unnecessary suffering. I could quote many other instances, but these two will suffice for my purpose. Now why does this happen? In my view it's because the experts think in terms of money rather than goods and accordingly put monetary arrangements first. That's precisely what they did in the Bretton Woods Agreement. This was a monetary agreement — which in our view should have been made after the vital problems of commercial policy had been settled. The London Chamber of Commerce in a pamphlet issued in December 1944, made this point quite

186

clear. It stated — that one of the purposes of the International Monetary Fund is 'To facilitate the expansion and balanced growth of international trade'. An international financial system could, of course, be used for this purpose and, in the Chamber's submission, it should be so used. In fact, however, the International Monetary Fund does nothing to bring pressure to bear on nations to balance their accounts with the world in terms of goods and services, its provisions are directed to ensuring a balance in money; and yet there can't, in the long run, be a balance in money unless there is a balance in trade. The Economic Reform Club and Institute also put this view to the Government. In our memorandum we pointed out our reasons for believing that the Bretton Woods Agreement would not work — and we particularly stressed the obligation under present conditions of creditor nations enabling debtor nations to discharge their indebtedness by accepting a surplus of imports over exports. As we pointed out, the Bretton Woods Agreement ignores this obligation — and actually strengthens the position of creditor nations while imposing penalties upon debtor nations. We stressed that so long as creditor nations won't recognise their obligation to accept an import surplus, there is little hope of facilitating the expansion and balanced growth of international trade. We suggested that the Bretton Woods Agreement showed that the gold mentality which we should long ago have outgrown is still with us.

Again — in July 1946 we made a submission on the White Paper called 'The proposals for consideration by an international conference on trade and employment.' Our submission was to the effect that non-discrimination would prove wholly unreasonable if it meant — as it has meant — curtailing trade with our Dominions and Colonies. We further pointed out that one of the necessary conditions of prosperous international trade was the assurance of stable and guaranteed markets, and that this would certainly not be achieved under the Bretton Woods proposals. These proposals, we argued, would inevitably lead to a desperate competition for world markets — with every nation struggling to avoid default, which — by the rules of the game — was certain to be the unfortunate fate of one or more of the nations concerned. We have also made other representations pointing out that the non-discrimination clause could not work, unless every country accepted the future obligation to buy as much as they sold.

Now I'm quoting these instances to you tonight, not because there is any pleasure in saying 'we told you so', but because I think it does entitle us to expect consideration of our views in the future.

It's obvious that the attempt which has been made to re-establish international free trade in money has failed as it was bound to fail under twentieth-century conditions. There are those who argue that the alternative is the introduction of bi-lateral barter arrangements. We claim that multi-lateral trade is quite possible — between all nations who are ready to accept trading goods for goods instead of goods for debt. It is, in fact, the only way of establishing a system which will ensure the highest standard of living for the peoples of all participating countries.

The first essential is that every nation should strive to develop its own natural resources to the full, arranging their internal economy so that the volume of purchasing power at all times balanced the supply of goods and services, instead of reducing the supply of goods and services to accord with inadequate purchasing power. This is fundamental — I can't stress the point too strongly — for it was our failure to carry out such a commonsense policy that caused much of our troubles in the years between the wars. Before this war — as you all know — we restricted output and scrapped capital equipment, and we did this because we failed to realise that the real wealth of the nation consisted of goods and services. As a result of the war we are now, of course, faced with the opposite position — but the same principle applies. This policy of equating consumption with production would enable us to maintain a stable internal general price level.

One of the difficulties in talking on these subjects is the definition of the terms used. For instance, the use of the term 'favourable balance of trade' to a situation where a nation is exporting more than it imports. Now the only sound reason for a nation to export is to enable it to pay for its necessary imports. The idea that a favourable balance of trade consists of exporting more than you import is obviously wrong, when you consider the situation in terms of real wealth, i.e., goods and services.

In the effort to export their unemployment problem nations strove for a so-called favourable balance and got those countries with the unfavourable balance into unpayable debt. In doing this, they perverted the real purpose of international trade, which should be mutual benefit. Trading for mutual benefit would create goodwill and friendship between nations, whereas trading for favourable balances creates fear and suspicion. In support, may I quote these words of a former US President, Mr Woodrow Wilson, 'Peace?' he said, 'why, my fellow-citizens, is there any man here, or any woman – let me say is there any child — who does not know that the seed of war in the modern world is industrial and commercial rivalry?'

What we must seek to do, therefore, is to establish an international trading system whereby a nation wishing to be paid for the goods it exports must take payment in the form of imported goods from other countries, and — if for some reason they don't want to do this — then they must forgo payment altogether after an agreed period had elapsed. There would be little difficulty in a nation accepting payment in goods, once it had established an internal economy under which its total purchasing power equalled the total volume of goods and services available.

In the inter-war period instead of taking payment for exports in the form of imports the foreign currencies the exporting nations received were sold for what they would fetch on the Foreign Exchange, so threatening the exchange rate of the buying country; or the proceeds were used — not to pay for imports — but to buy up the title deeds of the fixed assets of other countries, and they used the interest on those assets to buy up still more. This was certainly not the behaviour of good neighbours, and arising from it international trade was converted into financial and economic war between the nations.

It was Lord Nelson who wrote to the Sicilian Prime Minister — 'Nations are like individuals, make it to their interest to do what is right and they will do it'. We might take this advice to heart. The Bretton Woods scheme, which, as I have already said strengthens the position of creditor nations and imposes penalties on debtor nations, cannot be said to carry out this sound advice. And just look at the mess we are in as a result of continuing to work on these lines. We must set out to give nations no option, but to do what everybody agrees is the right thing, namely, to take goods and services in return for exports of goods and services. We must also make it impossible for one nation to upset the internal economy of others by selling their currencies on the foreign exchange. Each nation must be left entirely free to decide whether it wants to do a lot of foreign trade or a little foreign trade, but in so far as it stops imports by tariffs it stops its own exports to the same extent, unless it wishes to make a present.

We should suggest to the world that the terms and conditions governing international trade should follow this pattern. When you sell your goods to us we will chalk up on the board a credit in your favour, and you will clear that credit when you take our goods to that value. By giving you the credit we shall, in fact, have paid you, and it is for you to decide whether you wish to exercise your claim to goods or not. We propose to allow you to use the claim at any time and within a mutually agreed period — say seven years — and if you have not used the credit to buy goods by that time, we shall cancel the credit under a Statute of Limitations. We quite realise you may not want goods from us, and so, to enable you to have the benefit of multi-lateral trading we propose the setting up of an international Exchange to provide the machinery through which you will be able to exchange the claim you have on us, for claims on other countries.

After all, you know, this is only applying the same principle to nations which already applies to individuals. If I owe you a fiver and I give you a five pound note, I am not concerned whether you spend it. That is for you to decide. The same simple principle should apply to nations, and if a country doesn't wish to take imports in exchange for its exports, the only sensible way to deal with the matter is for the exporting nation to regard its exports as a gift to less fortunate nations, and here the matter should end.

In a talk of this nature I can't attempt to set out in detail the way in which such a system would work. As the aim and object is a state of equilibrium between nations, rates of exchange would need to be fixed, and once the true ratio had been agreed it should be maintained. Also we would want to use as much as possible the existing machinery, and the medium of bills of exchange, well understood by those engaged in the business of import and export, would easily lend itself to such a system. In fact, we are suggesting that international trade should be done by a system of contra account. There is no startlingly new principle involved in this. The larger proportion of trade between nations under any international system was on this basis. It was the outstanding balances, a small percentage of the total volume of world trade which caused all the trouble, and it is these balances with which we must deal by ruling that if a nation does not exercise its outstanding claims for goods and services within the agreed period the credit, under a Statute of Limitations, should be cancelled. As I have already indicated, an International Exchange would be set up, where participating nations could swop their claims at the conventionally fixed rate of exchange, and thus enable nations to trade on a multilateral basis.

I would suggest that in dealing with these economic questions we are not dealing with an abstract science, but with the way people and nations actually behave. It is important, therefore, to apply common sense to these problems rather than economic theory, which has so often failed us in the past. Each nation should be free to manage its own affairs, and what is supremely important if it fails to keep its balances in reasonable equilibrium with the rest of the world, the difficulties in which it would find itself would be entirely of its own making.

Now I know that many of you are thinking that the ideas I have outlined will not be readily acceptable by the main creditor nation today — the USA. In reply I would say that we have never put up these ideas to the people of the USA, and we can't say how they would react until we explain the ideas to them in understandable terms. My own belief is that these ideas are very much in line with the great democratic ideals and traditions of the United States. We do know what they did under the stress of war, when President Roosevelt, in his own words 'Cut out the dollar sign and removed the financial nonsense' by the introduction of lease-lend. In his American Commentary a few days ago Mr Joseph Harsch referred to "one arch conservative business man who is said to have made the plea to his Maker: 'Dear Lord, let us be a debtor nation again". That plea', said Mr Harsch, 'goes up from the heart of many an American, for being a debtor nation is something he understands.' This does not seem to me to indicate that the USA is thoroughly happy with the present state of affairs.

Judging by the magnificent response of the Dominions to the needs of Britain, there would be little difficulty in arriving at agreement with the Commonwealth and Empire. Other nations would no doubt wish to join with us. It is increasingly obvious that there is no future in the continuation of a system which automatically leads to unpayable indebtedness between nations. To maintain peace we must first establish it — for we can't maintain something which doesn't exist. Establish economic peace and much else follows. We can then set about providing guarantees that evilly disposed persons or nations shall not break it, with real hope of success, but so long as we tolerate a system of financial and economic war during so-called peace, it will be impossible to prevent outbreaks of physical violence.

The choice to be made in this matter of international financial machinery is crucial. It is a choice between peace and prosperity on the one hand, and on the other bitter trade war between nations, and history teaches us only too clearly how this usually ends.

INDEX